his legacy lives on

PRESS ASSOCIATION

'Pelé called me the greatest footballer in the world.
That is the ultimate salute to my life.'

Pelé

Edson Arantes do Nascimento

São Paulo, September 16th, 2010

I am honored to be invited to give a statement about a great player who was my idol, George Best, without a doubt one of the best football-artists we have ever had.

Unfortunately the new generations didn't have the pleasure and the opportunity to see him play personally as I did.

At that time television technology and the media in general were not so advanced as today and for this reason football lovers around the world didn't have the opportunity to watch him play.

The great football critics said that because of his technical skills he didn't seem like a European athlete but rather like a Brazilian athlete who danced the samba with the ball at his feet.

George Best until today is a footballer without comparison and his technical skills will never be forgotten.

May him rest in peace!

Edson Arantes do Nascimento - Pelé

'All the bad times cannot wipe away the good memories. Despite all the ups and downs, when I look back at my life as a whole, it is impossible for me not to feel blessed.'

his legacy lives on

THE GEORGE BEST FOUNDATION

ULSTER HISTORICAL FOUNDATION

Clay sculpture of the 'United Trinity' by sculptor
Philip Jackson MA FRBS FRSA, Spring 2008

First published 2011
Ulster Historical Foundation
49 Malone Road, Belfast BT9 6RY

ISBN 978-1-903688-92-2

Printed by Scotprint
Design by Dunbar Design

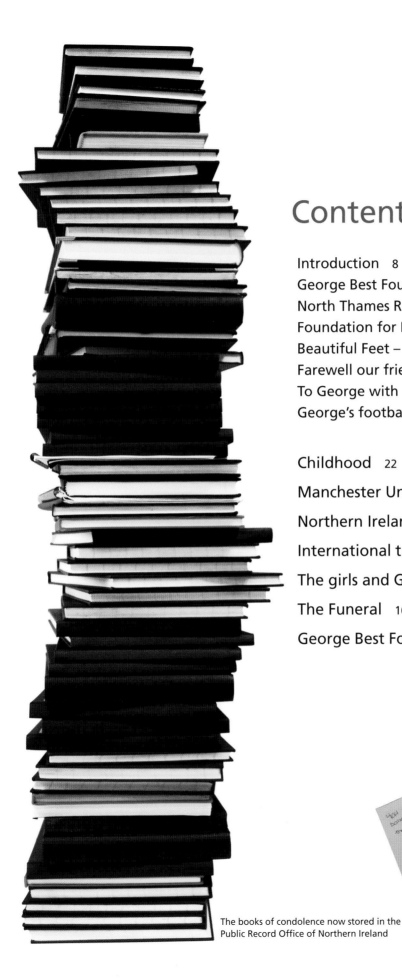

Contents

The books of condolence now stored in the Public Record Office of Northern Ireland

Introduction

The inspiration behind this outstanding tribute to George came from Mark Campbell and Jonathan Hamill, both employees of the Ulster Historical Foundation. Within hours of hearing the tragic news about George's death, Mark and Jonny made their way the Belfast City Hall, where books of condolence had been opened. They were amazed at just how many people had already arrived to pay their respects to George.

It rapidly became apparent just how many fans, not just Belfast-based, wanted to pay tribute to George in a way which was personal to each one of them. Many other books were opened by other bodies throughout Ireland. As well as the thousands of messages contained in the books, there were countless letters, poems, drawings and pictures which had been left at various locations. These included, the Cromwell Hospital in London, Old Trafford and the family home in Burren Way.

Mark and Jonny discussed how good it would be to have the most special tributes scanned and published in book form and with this in mind the Ulster Historical Foundation approached the George Best Foundation. Whilst it was a very difficult time emotionally, it was quickly decided that the charity would be honoured to be part of this unique project.

And so the task began. Every single tribute was carefully sifted through and the most poignant, sad or funny ones were selected. It was also apparent that tributes to the life of George extended way beyond his football skills and this book reflects many of those. The George Best Belfast City Airport, the George Best aeroplane, the Ulster Bank £5 note, George Best advertising deals, his honorary doctorate at Queen's University, the *Dancing Shoes* musical and many murals which replaced paramilitary style ones across Northern Ireland.

The book has been broken down into sections, dealing with George's childhood, his time at Manchester United, Northern Ireland, the international tributes he received, the women in his life and his funeral. Personal tributes have been written by Pelé, Sir Alex Ferguson, Sir Bobby Charlton, Pat Jennings, Eamonn Holmes, Graeme McDowell, Rory McIlroy, Gordon Taylor and Archbishop Desmond Tutu to name but a few.

What makes this book extra special is the inclusion of photographs of George which have never been published before as well as a simple painting which George did shortly before he passed away.

Enjoy browsing through this amazing tribute to one of the world's greatest and most loved sports personalities. It comes from those people who, despite George's ups and downs and his flaws, always stood by him.

It comes from the true fans.

Gevege Beff

FOUNDATION

George's life was blessed in one way, but blighted in another. He did not set out to be an alcoholic, but like hundreds of thousands all over the world, that's what he was fated to be. Over many years, despite many desperate and determined attempts to beat the illness, sadly George's alcohol addiction began to take a terrible toll on his health, culminating in the severe liver disease which finally necessitated a transplant.

George was cared for by a team of specialists led by the eminent consultant physician and haematologist, Professor Roger Williams CBE, one of the most highly respected specialists in the field of liver disease. George always referred to him affectionately as 'The Prof'.

George and the 'The Prof' shared more than just a doctor/patient relationship. A close bond developed between the pair during the period of George's initial treatment and this grew even stronger during the subsequent illness which led to his death. Ironically one of the aspects of George's life which never received much publicity over the years was his considerable work in raising funds for liver research.

In 2001 the George Best Appeal was set up and, both before and after his transplant, he devoted much time and effort raising awareness and raising funds for the Foundation for Liver Research.

He even addressed a House of Commons committee, speaking authoritatively and movingly about the effects of the terrible disease from which he was suffering. The fund meant a lot to him.

Some of the shirts left as a tribute to George after his death were donated to these children in Malawi

Remember support share

George Best Foundation and Manchester United Foundation players proudly display their number 7 jerseys at the George Best Memorial Trophy at Carrington, Manchester United Training Ground, 17 March 2010

10

He was particularly concerned that, despite the huge number of people in the United Kingdom suffering from the dreadful problem of alcoholism and the related illnesses caused by it, there was, and is, very little research being carried out into liver disease. It is no coincidence then that one of the aims of the George Best Foundation is to raise funds to help the vitally important research that meant so much to him. The George Best Foundation is honoured to have been able to donate, to date, £100,000 to the Foundation for Liver Research.

This is something of which George would undoubtedly have approved and would have been proud. But he would be proud and happy too of the impressive work the George Best Foundation does with young people. George's first love, undeniably, was football. But he loved and was extremely knowledgeable about sport in general. Reflecting this, the George Best Foundation has taken many positive steps to encourage young people to participate in a wide range of sports as well as providing vital education on health aspects, such as nutrition and vitally important drug and alcohol awareness. Most of our initiatives have taken place in Ireland and Great Britain, but we also support a number of international projects. George Best's enduring legacy will include all those young lives all over the world which have been helped and enhanced by the Foundation that carries his name.

George Best Foundation and Manchester United Foundation players: George Best Memorial Trophy; Carrington, Manchester United Training Ground, 17 March 2010

Norman McNarry, Paddy Crerand, Joseph Douglas, Alex Stepney, Matt Sellar; George Best Memorial Trophy; Carrington, 12 April 2011

MucH ADMIRED FOR
YOUR BATTLE ON ALCOHOLIC.
Also Your FootBall R. I. P.
Gone but not furgotten

ANONYMOUS

A genius at football you were
No one doubts that
A hard man on the bottle
No one questions that
A very special person in this life
All agree

Andy

The master taught football lessons on the
pitch. More importantly, he has taught me
the perils of the high life. And I needed it!
Thanks George for literally extending my life

PRIVATE & CONFIDENTIAL

Mr. R. Best
16 Burren Way
Belfast
BT6 0DW

1st December 2005

Dear Richard and Family

I would like to say again how sorry I am that your Son has died. I am very aware
that only a short time has passed since his tragic death and I hope that this letter
does not come as an intrusion. I would like to take this opportunity to offer my
sincere condolences to you and your family. Thank you for offering organ and
tissue donation at such a difficult and sad time.

As we discussed, we were sadly unable to proceed with organ and tissue
donation on this occasion. I know this news was disappointing for you all to hear,
it is important for you to know that it in no way detracts from the magnitude of
your offer. As you will only be too aware, it is only through the generosity of
families like yours that those on the waiting list continue to have hope.

Please do not hesitate to contact me at any time in the future should you have
any questions or simply wish to talk.

With kindest regards and warmest wishes

Julie Whitney
North Thames Regional Donor Transplant Coordinator

Chelsea and Westminster **NHS**
NHS Trust

From one alcoholic to another) no one can heart you anymore
God Bless

PROFESSOR ROGER WILLIAMS

Words spoken at funeral service

I quickly came to realise how much affection George attracted from all around the world. I attended meetings giving lectures on liver disease, but no one seemed to be a bit interested in what I had to say. All around the world, in South Africa, Australia, and the Middle East it was always 'How's George?' George mingled easily with people and had that lovely smile which seemed to put people at ease. After the transplant there were some very good times and he was very well indeed, but the temptations of life overtook him again. It is said that doctors shouldn't get too close to their patients. It's not that easy when that person is George Best.

'Hi Prof'. 'Hi George'. That's how it was.

Mr.and Mrs.Norman McNarry
Geworge Best Foundation
PO Box 972
Belfast BT4 9AJ

6th December 2006

Dear Barbara & Norman,

A great cheque and thank you. I do know how hard you have worked to achieve this and my task is to ensure that the very best research and benefit for the patients comes from it. In doing this I will be conscious all the time of why and how, remembering George's very definite wish to help others avoid the problems he was having and how he began the initial Appeal. We must all continue to work in his memory and I will look forward to meeting with you again in the New Year, possibly at the Old Trafford dinner in February. I hope by the middle of the year, at least, that we will be able to have some progress with the research that we can announce and the first George Best Fellow will take up his appointment here in the New Year.

Yours
Roger Williams

Professor Roger Williams, CBE
Director – Institute of Hepatology

Your life stolen because of one addiction you couldn't overcome. You will be missed - our Gorgie xo

At Peace now. Alcohol gave you the wings to fly. It then took away the sky....... Goodbye George. You wont be forgotten.

As a fellow transplant patient, I prayed for him ever day and know he's with god now xoxo.

BEAUTIFUL FEET
A SONG FOR GEORGE

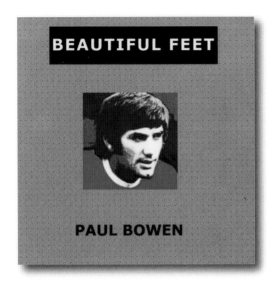

Belfast, December 3rd 2005 – Minutes after George Best's funeral cortège passed through the gates of Roselawn Cemetery, I sat down to write a song for my hometown hero, the world's greatest footballer. There were a lot of tears that day, not just in my home, not just in Belfast, but all over the world; for George's final homecoming had become our Diana moment, our JFK moment; one of those rare occasions when the world seems smaller, when people are drawn together through grief at the passing of a hero, through joy for the happiness that person gave them, in celebration of that person's life. We've all experienced those moments, and when you've lived through one, you'll never forget it. I tried that day, to capture George's moment. I think I did. It's called 'Beautiful Feet'.

As the gates of Roselawn closed behind him, a strange, warm sadness seemed to wrap itself around Belfast like a favourite scarf and I realised that George, in his moment, had achieved what legions of politicians, strategists, and public figures had for years failed to achieve – he truly had united a city divided.

Beautiful feet

Love like you've never seen
Brighter than our brighter dreams
Has come to our city streets
Thanks to your beautiful feet

Warm love so brilliant
Shines out of every window
Through the night 'til grey dawn's peep
Kisses your beautiful feet

You were the boy to behold
From Belfast streets to fields of gold
You lived them all, every teenage dream
You had the world at your beautiful feet

Manchester United
A city divided
It's a small step but one giant leap
Thanks to your beautiful feet

The game's a more beautiful place
All for the glory, the grace
When you defied gravity
With wings 'neath your beautiful feet

You were the boy to behold
From Belfast streets to fields of gold
You lived them all, every teenage dream
You had the world at your beautiful feet

You were the boy to behold
From Belfast streets to fields of gold
But now it's time, time, time to sleep
For the boy with the smile
and the beautiful feet

Sweet Georgie Best
You're home now, at rest
Long may the angels keep
Watch over your beautiful feet
In awe of your beautiful feet
Thank God for your beautiful feet

Farewell our friend

Poem read by Calum Best at his father's funeral

Farewell our friend, but not goodbye
Your time has come; your soul must fly
To dance with angels, find the sun
But how we'll miss our special one
He walks among us just a while
Weaved your magic, made us smile
Your life was full of light and tears
We lived it through you, through the years
The golden days they went so fast
The precious time, why can't they last?
So many loved you, did you know?
We were not ready to let you go
The stars from heaven are only lent
A gift from God, that's why they're sent
We won't forget our Belfast Boy
He filled our lives with so much joy
Your star will shine now in the sky
Farewell our friend, but not goodbye

To George with love

I cannot find adequate words to describe how honoured I am to be part of this wonderful tribute to you. The pride which I have always felt to have had you as my brother is immeasurable.

Little did I or the world realise what the future held for you when you left our home in Belfast as a scrawny fifteen-year-old. You went on to become the most naturally gifted player ever to grace a football pitch.

Sir Matt Busby was very quick to recognise that Bob Bishop was right when he described you as a 'genius' in that famous telegram.

'Don't try to coach him. Leave him alone. The boy is special,' is how Sir Matt put it.

And special you certainly were.

You were and still are loved by legions of fans from around the world. Those fans never let you down in life and continue to honour your memory in death.

I know without doubt that had Mum and Dad been alive today they would have wholeheartedly supported this project and like me, would have been privileged to contribute. Sadly that is not the case, so I have chosen a few words to reflect the love and pride which they both had for you.

Mum, who missed you more than words can say, spoke lovingly when she recalled the pain of being parted from you.

'I just saw him going out of my life. That was probably because he was my first-born. I pictured him going away to a country that he knew nothing about. I worried about how he would cope and what he would do because he was so shy and frail. It hurt me so much every time he came home and had to leave again and it was something which I never got used to.'

Dad, often found it difficult to express his emotions, but these words reveal how he felt. 'I don't say this often or to too many people, but I am proud of George. Deep down I am

George with his sister
Barbara, May 2002

so proud of him. Many a time I wanted to put my arms around him and make him better. When he died, I was so sad, but so proud and I just wanted to bring him home. I would love to see him walk through the door again.'

George, six years have passed since you left us, but you will forever be in our minds and in our hearts. You said shortly before your death that you wanted to be remembered for your football and if only one person thought you were the best player in the world, then that would be enough for you. How typical of you to be so humble.

One person? This book reflects the huge numbers of people who still remember you, not just for the football but for the person that you were. Despite your flaws, you had many shining qualities which endeared you to others.

If the important work of the George Best Foundation, which was set up in your memory, makes a difference to just one person's life, then that will do for me.

Love always,
Barbara

George in action for Northern Ireland, January 1973

George's football career and honours

22 May 1946–25 November 2005

Cregagh Boy's Club	Pre-1961 (rejected by Glentoran 1961)		
Manchester United	1963–74	470 appearances	179 goals
Jewish Guild South Africa	1974	5 appearances	not known
Stockport County	1975	3 appearances	2 goals
Cork Celtic	1975–76	3 appearances	0 goals
Fulham FC	1976–77	47 appearances	10 goals
Los Angeles Aztecs	1976, 1977, 1978	55 appearances	27 goals
Fort Lauderdale	1979, 1980	29 appearances	6 goals
Hibernian	1979–80	22 appearances	3 goals
San Jose Earthquakes	1979–80, 1981	56 appearances	21 goals
AFC Bournemouth	1983	5 appearances	0 goals
Brisbane Lions	1983	4 appearances	0 goals
Tobermore United	1984	1 appearance	0 goals
Northern Ireland International Team	1964–78	37 appearances	9 goals

1966–67 First Division Champions
1968 European Cup Champions
1968 European Footballer of the Year
1968 Football Writers' Player of the Year

Childhood

A minute's applause from the heart of the terrace

Parry Maguire

All football legends would prefer
To go back to their maker
With the sounds of terrace applause
Ringing in their ears and boots
As opposed to the silence

George Best's skill as a footballer
Was a thing of beauty
And I mourned the passing of his genius long ago
Now is the appropriate time
To applaud that genius.

Especially those who were privileged
To have witnessed the man
On the football pitch
Where he touched our hearts
Perhaps just fleetingly with his sublime gifts
As he raced past

With a swivel of his hips and a twinkle of his toes
Along the touchline …
A part of my childhood slipped away
And I'm not ashamed to say that yesterday
I shed tears for the loss of both

CHILDHOOD DAYS

First known photo of George taken
17 September 1946 aged 4 months

The war in Europe had just ended, food was rationed and money was tight. But nothing could disguise Dickie Best's happiness when he married his first love Ann Withers on 30 June, 1945. They both wanted a family and when their first-born George arrived just eleven months later on 22 May, 1946, they were overjoyed. Little did they know then what the future held for their east-Belfast working-class family and for their much loved son.

Remarkably George walked at just ten months old. By the time he was only fifteen months, he was already displaying skill with a football. One day his dad took a snapshot of the toddler in typical pose with his head down over the ball, totally concentrating and looking completely natural. That treasured, grainy, old black and white snap is the first photograph of George Best demonstrating his football skills to the world.

In January 1949, the family moved to Burren Way in the Cregagh estate and it was in this street and in this estate that George practised and honed his skills as a player. From the time that he first kicked a football, George was seldom seen without one at his feet. He was a happy, contented, exceptionally bright boy who did well at school.

But football was his passion.

George attended Nettlefield Primary School, where he barely had time for lunch as all he wanted to do was play football. In 1957, after passing his qualifying exam, George went to the local grammar school, Grosvenor High. But to his great dismay, football was not part of the school curriculum. George actually excelled at rugby in Grosvenor. But it wasn't for him.

Moved by his pleas his parents eventually agreed to transfer him to Lisnasharragh Secondary School where once again he was able to play his beloved sport.

George played for Cregagh Boys' Club and it was here that he was discovered by the Manchester United talent scout Bob Bishop. Bishop is the man who famously sent a telegram to Matt Busby which simply but prophetically informed him: 'I think I've found you a genius'. At just fifteen years of age, George left his native Belfast to become one of the most talented football players of all time.

This section of the book contains many touching tributes, not just from children who never even saw him play, but from adults with their own fond memories of how George Best had an impact on their lives. It is a moving and true reflection of the high esteem in which George is still held by people right across the generations.

George's Mum enjoyed a very close relationship with her own parents, sisters and brother, who lived in Donard Street in east Belfast. Consequently, from an early age, George spent a lot of time there. It was in Donard Street that these photographs, including that now very famous one of George at fifteen months old kicking a ball, were taken.

George aged 15 months with Aunt Joan

George aged 18 months with Aunt Minty

Dressed to kill for a trip to the seaside. Aunts Joan and Georgie with George and Cousin Louis, Bangor, 7 July 1954

Proud Mum and Dad with George holding the Football Writers' Association Player of the Year Award 1968. Brother Ian and twin sisters Grace and Julie

25

Cregagh Boys' Club

Two of George's awards from Cregagh Boys' Club

I have come a long way from the days when I played in east Belfast for Cregagh Boys' Club, when folk dismissed my chances by saying 'there was more fat on a chip'. Old Trafford was a much bigger stage, but I was playing the same game, in a situation that was beyond my wildest dreams.

George

May the
Warm memories you have
bring you strength from day to day
And may time find a way
to heal your loss

With Sympathy

With Deepest Sympathy

May you find peace
and comfort
knowing that thoughts
are with you

from the staff and pupils
of Knockbreagh High School

The loss of an amazing talent

Northern Ireland Youth Team 1963. The match versus Wales at Aberystwyth was played four days before George's seventeenth birthday

WALES

RIGHT   LEFT

C. J. Park
(Swansea Town)

A. Lucas (Capt.)   D. P. Jones
(Wrexham)   (Caernarvon Town)

W. R. Davies   J. Smith   A. Pierce
(Glanrhyd)   (Rhos Aelwyd)   (Caersws)

R. I. Hughes   D. Evans   M. Jones   D. Pugh   B. Lewis
(Ruabon G.S.)   (Berriew)   (Llanidloes)   (Newport C.)   (Cardiff City)

REFEREE :
Mr. J. W. PATTERSON,   LINESMEN :
Bothwell, Scotland.   Mr. G. L. EVANS, Llandyssul.
                             Mr. D. T. DAVIES, Lampeter.

W. Reid   G. Best   D. Guy   J. Anderson   R. Warburton
(Linfield) (Manchester U.) (Linfield) (Distillery) (Glentoran)

D. Watson   R. J. Napier   J. Nicholl (Capt.)
(Glentoran)   (Bolton Wanderers)   (Coleraine)

H. McCurley   T. Corbett
(Linfield)   (Ballyclare C.)

J. Stokes
(P.O.S.C.)

LEFT   RIGHT

IRELAND

27

Northern Ireland.

Remember him For his Football. George best.

Man u.

by ROSS

by Ross

Your inspiration will live forever, in the proud faces of the Lisnasharragh pupils. Everytime a ball is kicked, <u>you</u> are in their hopes and dreams, <u>you</u> are the spark in their eyes.

Head of P.E.

With deepest sympathy to the Best Family. George's achievements are an inspiration to all Lisnasharragh pupils

Vice-principal (Acting)

It was a dream come true for me.

It would have been for any kid. At fifteen years old, for someone to come up to you and ask if you wanted to play for Manchester United, you can't truly describe the feeling.

I used to dream about taking the ball round the keeper, stopping it on the line and then getting on my hands and knees and heading it into the net. When I scored against Benfica in the European Cup final, I nearly did it, but then I chickened out as I might have given the boss a heart attack.

George

George training January 1964

George visiting John Doherty as a child in hospital and left, John with the signed shirt given to him by George.

John Doherty

It was an occasion which John Doherty will treasure for the rest of his life. It was the moment that he received a gift from George Best. It was George's very own football shirt which he had worn in a match against Scotland on 21 October 1967 at Windsor Park, when George put in one of his most memorable performances in a green jersey.

John had been ill and was in the Belfast Children's Hospital. A friend of his, Dr Malcolm Brodie had told George that John was ill and asked if he would send an autograph for him. George, however, went one step further than that and decided to visit John instead.

John recalls, 'George dropped a small paper bag on the bed and said "there's a little extra present for you, but don't open it until I'm gone." I think he had only been gone a couple of seconds before I tore the bag open, expecting to find some sweets. To my great surprise and delight, it contained his shirt from the previous day's match. It's very rare that you get to meet your hero in life. It's not that often that your dreams come true, but that day George made my dreams come true.'

Thank you George.

George encourages potential young players, 1970

Johnny, Belfast

As a child I saw you play at Windsor Park and you changed how I viewed the world and you inspired me in so many ways. I had George Best boots, pyjamas, badges and posters and was a member of the fan club. You were a very, very special human being.

Julian, Nottingham

You were a real genius and my hero as a boy and now part of my childhood has gone forever, but never forgotten. Just pure class and that will never die. Please take care of him he really is that special.

Aaah! :(

His faith will allways be thier.

2005. By Jennifer age 6 from Worsley. Goerge Best Sunday 27th November.

Gole

ULSTER HAS
MANY HEROES
BUT YOU WERE A
TRUE LEGEND
SIMPLY THE BEST
BETTER THAN
ALL THE REST
FROM GEORGIA
WEST AGED 4
NITE NITE
GEORGE
XXXXXXXXXX

NORTH
IRE

Tribute, Burren Way

Mike, Cardiff

As a boy I supported Watford and still do. We played Manchester United in 1969 in the 3rd round of the Cup at Old Trafford. We drew 1–1 and I went to the replay at our place. Manchester United beat us 2–0. A little boy's heart should have been broken, but it wasn't. My lasting memory to this day was wonderment at seeing an absolute genius at work. God rest and bless you, you were special.

Wayne, Doncaster

As a young boy I can always remember David Coleman saying in the 1970s, 'Let your son stop up late and watch this genius in action'. When I watched it, George beat four or five people and slotted the ball in the net. Bestie was the greatest and is a hero that has passed away.

Dear George,

Although I was never privileged enough to see you play, my Dad was and he has told me that no-one could touch you.

The clips that survive are the image of a genius that will last for generation after generation. You had a truly special talent.

I have been lucky enough to see the likes of Keane, Cantona and Schmeichel play in the red shirt, and these are giants that walk in the footsteps carved by your generation.

Long Live George, your talent will never be forgotten.

Alex Trembath.

My dad drew this

Hi my name is Kyle Reid. I am from Northern Ireland (Belfast). I herd you were sick and I thought of writing to you. I also play For a Football team called Donegal Celtic and I am number 11. I support Manchester United and I have all of their kits and I have a few of their kits up on my wall. I have been to one of their matches against Blackburn Rovers. I am 11 years old and I am number 11 For my Football team. My favourite food is Pizza. I am doing my 11 plus on the 25th of November so wish me good luck!

Hope
    you
        Get
            well   soon

Lots of Love

Kyle Reid

To

George best
Hope you get well

...HEAL QUICKLY!

Cant wait till you get out of hospital

Lots of Love

Kyle Reid
I'm your no. 1 Fan

I hear you haven't been too well...

During George's time in the Cromwell Hospital, he received countless get well cards and messages, many of which were read out to him. During the last weeks and days of his life, a lot of very moving and special messages arrived. One in particular, from an eleven-year-old boy from Belfast called Kyle Reid, an ardent Manchester United fan, struck a chord with George's sister Barbara and for some reason she slipped the card into her bag. At that stage, neither Barbara nor Kyle knew how things would turn out.

When George passed away, the family were very aware of the tremendous amount of support which the fans had given to George. He respected the support which had been given to him throughout his entire life, through the good times and bad by the many genuine fans who loved him in return. With this in mind, it was decided that ten members of the public, who had waited patiently for hours in the cold and rain to pay tribute to their hero would be invited to the ceremony inside Stormont.

It then became crystal clear why Barbara had kept the card safely tucked away. There was an address for Kyle, but no telephone number, so the local police were on hand and very kindly called at his home and left a message that George's sister wanted to speak to Kyle. To his and his Mum Geraldine's shock and pleasure they were both invited to join the family at George's funeral service.

Following the service Kyle said, 'I felt really lucky. George Best's sister thanked me for coming and said she hoped I would never forget that day. There's no chance of that'.

Geraldine said, 'Kyle is very thoughtful but we never expected this to happen. We are truly honoured for a day that we will never forget'.

Michael

Hi George, I hope you are feeling better. My Dad says you were the best ever. I never got to watch you myself but he skipped school to watch you beat Benfica at Wembley. By the way, my Mum reckons she went on a date with you. Her name was Helen, long ginger hair and lived in Chorlton-cum-Hardy. Do you remember? I'm kind of hoping I'm your love child!! Only joking. God bless George.

Please get well soon.

Original jersey which George exchanged with Antonio Simoes, European Cup Final 1968

Roy, Fareham

When listening to the tributes to George last night on talkSPORT my six-year-old saw a tear run down my cheek. He said, 'Are you crying because of that footballer that died'? I said 'yes son'. After a short silence he said softly with his head low, 'he must have been a very special man'. There was nothing more to say. Thank you George for everything.

Rest in peace now Belfast boy.

A tribute to

George Best

This book contains messages of condolence received on the talkSPORT website from the followers who appreciated the genius of George Best.

George signs autographs for young fans Harold Dennis and friend Roy Clark, May 1969

And here are three of the exciting drawings being reproduced in George Best On The Ball. In all it contains 30 such strips, backed up with action photographs illustrating similar situations in actual matches.

Best Way Forward, 2008, sponsored by George Best Foundation

Georgie Best – Superstar

George, I wear my Manchester United kit with pride. Although I never saw you play, I have seen you at Old Trafford watching the games and I watch you on DVDs. I continue to learn so much from your shooting, passing and dribbling the ball. Your life has been cut short, but your memories will always be with me.

Guy aged 12: Manchester United LMTB Holder

John Pilkington

Just wanted to say what effect George Best had on us kids who grew up in the 60s.

Everyone wanted to be George Best and unfortunately this used to lead to quite a few arguments. To overcome this we would take turns and it was the best feeling in the world when it was your turn. In reality, we all know there was only one George Best and we will continue to mourn his loss every single day.

You were an inspiration to a generation.

Rebecca, Bangor

I may be only 16 years of age, but I know that George Best was an inspiration, a legend and a hero to many fans. I'm glad he was brought home to Belfast, to his roots and his homeland. He will be sorely missed throughout the world, but never forgotten here in Northern Ireland.

GARY HANCOCK

Best Way Forward, 2008, sponsored by George Best Foundation

Grace

How many families can claim to have had a brother and a sister play on a Northern Ireland International football team? I don't know the statistics, but what I can say is the Best family is certainly one of them. Not only was I very proud to have played for the Northern Ireland Ladies team from 1979–81, but very honoured to have worn the number eleven shirt, the same as George. As a young boy, George's favourite team was Wolves and by coincidence, I wore the Wolves strip when I played for the Post Office Ladies team, aged 15.

I fondly remember George's Testimonial match at Windsor Park in Belfast in 1988. George still had charisma and showed a lot of his unique skills. I cried that evening, not just for the pride which I felt for George, but for the one person who was not there to share it – our Mum.

Next to our beautiful daughter Ashleigh's death, George's passing was the hardest thing which I've ever had to deal with. George loved children, especially Ashleigh, describing her as 'the best little kid I ever met'.

Memories of my brother will always be precious and special. He was a unique person, witty and generous. I will always be so proud and count it as a privilege to have had George as my big brother and to have been a small part of his life.

Lots of love
Grace

George's sister Grace with son Andrew, George and Calum

Dear Bobby, Thank-you very much for inviting us to come to Eddie Irvine Sports yesterday, we had a great day out and enjoyed it very much. I now know how to play a bit of football. The bouncy castles were great fun! The lunch was nice too. We are very grateful towards the George Best Foundation for paying for us to have a fab day out. The talk was very good and it was exciting to meet a footballer who plays for Glentoran.

Yours (Sea) Sincerely

Rebekah.

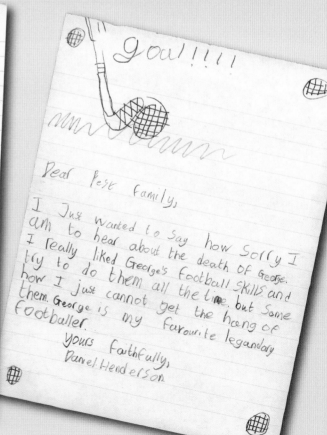

goal!!!!!

Dear Pest Family,

I Just wanted to say how sorry I am to hear about the death of George. I really liked George's football skills and try to do them all the time but some how I just cannot get the hang of them. George is my favourite legandary footballer.

Yours faithfully,
Darrel Henderson.

Dear Sam,

I enclose signed photo as requested.

Shall keep your letter as I'm quite a fan of yours — and your Aunt's — on the TV. I think you are quite right about having a proper egg breakfast every day to be your best (no pun intended!) and always have one myself. I'm sure eggs help me keep fit and in trim. Also I don't get that sinking feeling before dinner-time.

Yours,

George Best

E for B and George Best!

All the Best! George

Dear mr. Best
I am really really sorry to hear that your son has died. So I am trying to make you feel better by writing you this. And I really really like football your son was one of my favourite player.

yours sincerely
Matthew crossland

Dear Mr. Best

I was sorry to hear about your son george. He was the Best footballer in the word. I know you will miss hem very much but now he is with his mum. and I am sure he is the Best footballer in God's house. So take care

your sincerly
Margie McNicholl

AS A SCHOOL DINNER LADY IN 1968, I GOT THE CHILDREN TO EAT THEIR FOOD BY TELLING THEM THAT COOKSTOWN SAUSAGES WERE ON!!

Chloe   good bye Mr george !

George, I have great memories of you but one goes back to 1963 when I ate jam sandwiches for two weeks so I could save my dinner money to buy a Man U strip for 9/6d! Had to confess all to my mother as I wanted her to sew the magic '7' on the back. She forgave me for missing my school dinners. Thanks for everything, George.

Goodbye old school friend
Seems like yesterday you
won "Sports boy of the year"!"

When people think of Northern Ireland
people think of:

1. the riots
2. the sights
3 George Best

his skills will live on

Granny Withers and Aunt Lily with the clan on summer holidays, July 1956

GRAEME   (BANGOR)

I WAS BORN IN 1960 BUT IT WAS NOT UNTIL 25 NOV 2005 THAT MY CHILDHOOD DIED. YOU WERE MY HERO, ARE MY HERO AND WILL BE MY HERO TILL THE DAY I DIE. WE ALL LOVE YOU AND ARE PROUD OF YOU - YOU WILL ALWAYS BE REMEMBERED - GOD BLESS.

MARK CAMPBELL   My childhood hero, never to be forgotten a true legend.

Thanks for making our son Christopher feel so special when you came over to him in Manchester August 2000. He died the following year but he was proud to have met George Best even though was only 16. The Best Footballer was so a very special Person.

Dear Barbara,
I think I am the best George Best fan for numerous reasons.

Firstly, when i was in year 5 the whole class had to choose an independant Project about a famous person or legend. every one chose a person like Ronaldo or Beyonce however i chose george best. Everyone thought i was a bit wierd but i didnt care as i knew Best was the best. Also every one wrote a short project but i wrote a long one because George best is so fascinating.

Secondly, not long ago my mum bought us a dog coincidently he is an irish staffordshire bull terrier who likes football we couldnt think of a name then it came to me "Bestie". Also when me and my brother are playing football the dog always steals the ball off us and we never get it back just like george and the other players.

Finaly, at my grandmas house we redecorated one of her best rooms into a room all dedicated to George Best it has loads of pictures and a pillow with a picture of george on it. When i sleep there we watch films about him on a night time. Also i read some books about him my favourite books are Blessed, hard tackles, Dirty best, george best Celebrations, the good the bad and the bubbly, our george, and the autobiography of george Best my favourite DVD's are genious mavric legend, george best the genious and the legend, best intentions Bests view.

thank you for taking the time to read my letter

love Charlie Quickfall
xxx

The best thing about my 70's childhood Northern Ireland people were fabulas despite those tratted times and you were the epitomy of that.

George, Carol, Uncle George and cousin Louis, July 1956

The Founder of the Theatre of dreams

Pro-Excel Move It Show

3 December 2007

The second anniversary of George's passing was marked in a very special way. Two years to the day since the world was gripped by the images of his funeral, more than 70 young people from his homeland followed in the footsteps of the Belfast Boy to Manchester. It was there that they would perform a stunning dance show which would commemorate the life of George, who had been one of the most charismatic sporting figures the world had ever known.

The 'Move It' project is designed, much like the work of the George Best Foundation, to use the power of football and other sports to develop healthy living and fitness in young people.

Over 400 school pupils auditioned for just one of 70 places in the project, which was totally cross-denominational and socially very diverse. Paddy Crerand who was on hand to chat to the students said, 'George did more than most to bridge the divide in Belfast'. Part of the process of the project, included the input from the performers to choose the theme and purpose of the show. Unanimously, the students wanted to dedicate their performance to George.

Seventy happy students flew on the George Best Plane from the George Best Belfast City Airport to perform on an enormous purpose built stage, at the famous Trafford Centre Shopping Mall. The show itself was fabulous. The music to which the students performed was chosen to best describe George and was merged with commentary from different times and places in George's life and career. The show opened to 'Georgie, the Belfast Boy', followed by Bonnie Tyler's' 'Hero' and then Queen's 'Don't Stop Me Now'. Poignantly, the finale saw the students form a huge GB to a recording of 'You Raise Me Up', which was performed so beautifully at George's funeral service.

Whilst many tributes have been paid to George throughout his life and career, this one certainly falls into the unique and memorable category.

MANCHESTER EVENING NEWS

George returns to Belfast to present awards, September 1964

Jade, Manchester

I never really knew a lot about George Best but did know he was a really great man. I wasn't around when he was at his peak as I am only 14. My dad said he was the greatest man he ever shook hands with and said George was so polite that he bought my dad a drink. When I went to Old Trafford to see the things people had laid out for him, it really just hit me what a great man he was and that is why he will never be forgotten. I felt that he was there that night and it just made me cry. I read on a shirt that "he came from heaven, now he's going back". I think that is amazing, all the love that was showed then. As I laid my candle my dad started to cry and so did the man next to him so that set me off again! To George's family all I have to say is take care and realise how much George's story could help others. We will never forget you!

Rest in peace George Best, the Belfast Boy.

Dennis, Bedfordshire

I have spent a lifetime explaining to others why a lad living in the East End of London supports Manchester United. The reason is and always was that Georgie Best plays for them. Thanks George. You are the greatest player these shores will ever see.

Hughie, Hertfordshire

George was not only the most naturally gifted player I ever saw but was genuinely kind-hearted.

My late son Liam was one of many children receiving treatment at the Central Middlesex Hospital in the late 1980s. George spent two hours of unreported time with them during which he was an absolute gentleman and charmer with the children, their parents and staff.

Jack, Berkshire

Hi, I am Jack and I am only 13 years old. I wasn't fortunate enough to see George Best play but I had always heard he was rated with Maradona and Pelé. At first I didn't know what all the fuss was about. Over the past few days I have watched endless clips of George in his prime and it did not take long for me to realise he was simply the Best player I have ever seen play football. Now I am inspired to become the Best player I can be. A true Legend who has thrilled me. Thanks again George.

Alex, Southampton

I was told the sad news just before I collected my six-year-old son from school. We got in my car and I could not hold back my tears. My son said 'what's wrong dad?' I explained that like he had super heroes, I had mine and it was George who died today. He asked me if he was strong and I told him very, he then asked if he could fly and I also told him yes he could fly past the very best. He said 'don't worry dad he can still be your hero'. Thanks for giving me so much enjoyment.

George Best

born died
1946 — 2005

A hero to the forrell family from Dublin

A Legend

MANCHESTER UNITED DAYS

George joined Manchester United as an amateur in 1961 and within two years he had made his first team debut against West Bromwich Albion. Although George was very much the new boy on the block, he was quickly to become a top flight player. In 1966, in a match against the mighty Benfica in the Stadium of Light, George virtually had the game sealed when he scored twice within twelve minutes. He returned to Manchester dubbed 'El Beatle' and from then on, George's life changed from being simply a footballer to becoming a worldwide celebrity.

In 1968 George was awarded the Football Writers' Player of the Year, being the youngest person at the time to win this award. Just two weeks later, George was to be instrumental in helping Manchester United and Sir Matt Busby realise their dream by becoming the first English club to win the European Cup. Following this, George was nominated European Player of the Year. Quite an achievement for a twenty-two-year old.

During his career with the club, George made 470 appearances, scoring 179 goals. It is very apparent just how many people support Manchester United because of George, a tradition which has been passed down through the generations.

Dr Malcolm Brodie MBE

Well over 40 years ago, two youngsters walked into my office at the *Belfast Telegraph*. One wore a Lisnasharragh School blazer, the other was an exuberant chirpy little fellow. They were photographed holding a ball – just two of the many kids with stars in their eyes, about to realise their dream of entering English football.

George was the ultimate genius.
Remember him for his goals, incomparable artistry and the joy he gave to millions.

George with Eric McMordie, 1961
Preparing to leave for Old Trafford, George
wears his school blazer and prefect's badge

BELFAST TELEGRAPH

Manchester United

Poetry in motion　David Brailsford

Best from Charlton
through to Law
back to Best
　　　　United score

sublime for those
who watched in awe
a talent
millions would adore.

receive the ball
upon his chest
hold it, keep it
sweet caressed

with two feet
so completely blessed
raw talent
that was Georgie Best

the genius
of whom I speak
with pedigree
of rich mystique

untouchable
whilst at his peak
a football icon
　　　　quite unique

'I think I have found you a genius'

That's how local football scout Bob Bishop famously put it in a telegram message to Sir Matt Busby after he had watched George, a scrawny wee lad, playing for Cregagh Boys Club. Others had dismissed George as being too small. 'He'll never make the grade,' they said.

Initial trials with Manchester United were set up for both George and another Belfast lad, Eric McMordie, and in the summer of 1961 at the tender age of just fifteen, a very shy George left for Manchester. Initial homesickness nearly pulled the plug on both of their careers, however, and just twenty-four hours after arriving at Old Trafford, two very unhappy teenagers fled back to their homes in Belfast. In that very short space of time though, Sir Matt had also seen enough to convince him that Bob Bishop had indeed found him a genius. He contacted Dickie Best, George's father. But it was George himself who made the decision. A fortnight later the young Belfast boy returned to Manchester and his destiny.

Less than two years later, on his seventeenth birthday on 22 May, 1963, George signed professionally for Manchester United.

His football career took George to far off places and glittering heights. As the newest 'Busby Babe', he quickly became a star and an inspiration in the Manchester United team still recovering from the terrible memories of the Munich air crash of 1958.

On so many occasions he dazzled the fans with his repertoire of feints and swerves as he baffled, bewildered and literally ran rings around his opponents.

The Welsh International Graham Williams famously spoke for all those run ragged on the field just trying to keep up with George. 'Stand still son so I can have a look at your face', he said. 'All I've seen all day is your backside disappearing up the touchline'.

In 1966, Manchester United and George gave one of their best and most memorable performances against the mighty Benfica in the quarter finals of the European Cup in Lisbon. Despite having been told by Sir Matt to 'keep it tight', George scored twice within twelve minutes. The final score was 5–1.

As the team touched down back home, George, with a sombrero on his head, was snapped by waiting photographers as he left the plane. 'El Beatle' the headlines called him. Papers couldn't get enough of him. Stories about him dominated not just the sports section but the front pages too.

George continued to light up Manchester United both at home and abroad. In 1968, ironically once again against Benfica, he made Sir Matt's dream come true. With time in the game running out, he took control of the ball, received it with his back to the goal, drifted past his marker, past the goalkeeper and casually rolled the ball into the net. George was voted European Player of the Year as well as English Football Writers' Association Footballer of the Year.

With his combination of good looks, charisma and sporting genius, George Best had become the first superstar of football.

BELFAST TELEGRAPH

George on Sir Matt

He can remain aloof and yet human.
He can tear us apart and still command respect
He can praise us and we know he is genuine
He can advise us and we know there is no dark motive

George and Sir Matt at the 'Best Testimonial' banquet.
Europa Hotel, Belfast, August 1988

Brian Robson with Sir Alex Ferguson, 1 December 2005

Manchester United versus West Bromwich Albion

First home game at Old Trafford following George's death. Ironically George's debut game was against West Bromwich Albion on 14 September 1963

'This player could be the next George Best,' or 'He is the new George Best,' are almost standard clichés I have had to deal with in my twenty-five years with Manchester United as manager. If only it were true, but I have to deal with reality and it just won't happen. As much as I would love to have a player who could be compared to the Belfast lad, I am just happy to have had Ryan Giggs for twenty years or so and he has been a wonderful player.

I first set eyes on George in a full game when Ireland played Scotland at Windsor Park and he was unbelievable, unplayable and uncatchable. It was one of the greatest performances I have seen from a Scottish opponent. Our left back that day was the Celtic player Tommy Gemmill, who was one of the best full backs in the game. George turned him inside out. Tommy was essentially an attacking player, but George was back tackling like a defender himself! That day has never left my mind and of course George went on to become one of the greatest players of all time in an era when we had the luxury of Di Stefano, Cruyff, Pelé and Eusebio. What a galaxy of stars they were! People will always ask the questions, 'why was he so good, what were his main strengths, etc' and of course all sorts of opinions are given.

My assessment of George is this. He was quick and elusive; he had good feet and had what was essential to a great player, balance and courage. It was his courage that most impressed me, as when defenders were kicking him all over the pitch, he always got the ball and went back for more.

He was not going to let anyone stop him from displaying his skill and when you think of some of the defenders in those days, you have to admire that bravery. He set down the template for greatness through his courage and any budding young star would be advised to follow that example. If you have talent and skill, don't let anyone take it away from you.

I would also like to pay tribute to the George Best Foundation for all of the work it carries out on his behalf. The charity has already given considerable funding to deserving causes and, with your support; it can carry on with this funding.

Alex Ferguson

Sir Alex Ferguson CBE

BELFAST TELEGRAPH

George and Bobby Charlton in action against Chelsea's John Hollins

Sir Bobby Charlton   Manchester United

George Best was a marvel with the ball and without the ball. A dream footballer who was confident in ability with supreme control at pace, and brave in the tackle when needed. He had a priceless vision to see openings before anyone else and was always aware of where his players were. He scored goals which were unique and he used to take some big hits from defenders who had no other way of stopping him.

Once at the Stretford End he scored a goal as I was screaming for the ball and although I was in a better position I never got his pass. I couldn't complain as he confounded me by smashing the ball into the top corner of the opponent's goal. Better not worry about it though and just enjoy being there to see it.

Whenever football fans debate who was the best, George in a lot of people's eyes would be top of the list.

Manchester United's glorious history has been created by people like George. Anyone that witnessed what he could do on the pitch wished they could do the same. He enriched the lives of anyone that saw him play.

MIRROR GROUP

Gordon Taylor   Bolton Wanderers

I was born in Ashton-under-Lyne, near Manchester, so it was only natural that in the 50s, together with my friends, we were football mad and made regular trips to see Bert Trautmann's Manchester City and Manchester United's Busby babes.

After having a trial for England schoolboys I was approached by a number of clubs, including Manchester United, but signed for Bolton Wanderers as they had a reputation for bringing through all their own players and the Chief Coach, George Taylor had been to the same school as my Dad and provided us with tickets to watch games so I signed for Bolton.

Imagine my feelings when, in the 1963/64 season, I was selected for the first team with Francis Lee for the game at Old Trafford in the autumn. The place was buzzing and the team talk centred around our defence trying to contain the strike force of Bobby Charlton, Denis Law and David Herd and hardly any mention was made of two young boys from Northern Ireland on both wings.

In the days before substitutes, unfortunately, I clashed with Denis Law and those famous elbows broke my nose and I had to come off the pitch to be tended by the Manchester United Club Doctor who asked whether I wanted to go to hospital to have it reset or grit my teeth and have it done then. I chose to grit my teeth. The Manager came into the dressing room and asked how I felt and, whilst I was groggy, I said I wanted to get back onto the pitch as quickly as possible. The Manager, Bill Ridding did not seem so sure and when I asked him what the problem was he said well the fact was that we were 5–0 down and it may look better if we only had ten men! When I asked who had done the damage he referred to one of the two young wingers who was from Northern Ireland.

On the right wing had been Willie Anderson, but on the left wing had been George Best who had run riot scoring two goals and laying on the rest. I think from then on George would never have been left out of any pre-match team talk as he went on to become one of the finest players ever to grace the football field and I just feel privileged to have played against him.

I played against him in later years for Blackburn Rovers against Fulham and for Vancouver Whitecaps against Los Angeles Aztecs and whilst he retained all his skills even in his later years, nothing could surpass the energy, vitality and skill of those early years.

PROFESSIONAL FOOTBALLERS' ASSOCIATION

Chief Executive: Gordon Taylor OBE, BSc (Econ), Hon DArt, Hon MA, FRSA

When I think back, they were probably the happiest days of my life. Talk about fulfilling a dream. Those days were just pure perfection. I was playing against and with great players. In 1968 I was voted European Footballer of the Year, the third player from United to win it in five years, following Denis in 1964 and Bobby in 1966.

George Best 2002

The first time I saw George play was in the first team and it was such a surprise. The lad had the ability to control the ball and turn in such sharp circles. He could turn on a sixpence. You couldn't teach anybody to do what George did.

Sir Bobby Charlton

Once Bestie got on that pitch, I suppose it was like a pop singer when he goes on stage in front of thousands of fans. When George went on a run, he was absolutely superb, riding tackle after tackle.

Denis Law

Johnny Giles   Manchester United Leeds United Republic of Ireland

My first contact with George was when he arrived at Old Trafford as a shy, quiet fifteen-year-old kid from Northern Ireland. I was twenty then and had just broken into the first team at Manchester United. In 1963, we won the FA Cup beating Leicester City in the final at Wembley. The start of the following season, I played alongside George Best twice in the reserves. I played on the right wing with George on the left. By Christmas, he had broken into the first team at Manchester United and by the end of that season, he was a superstar. In my view, George was simply a genius with his incredible balance off both sides that made him virtually impossible to mark.

There had never been a phenomenon like George Best in football before and I think it took everyone at Old Trafford by surprise. Yes, you had the likes of Stanley Matthews and Tom Finney, but they were spoken of purely in football terms. George was the first football superstar in Britain who was loved not only for his sheer football genius, but also his looks and lifestyle. It was a changing time in Britain and I think George was a victim of his time, almost a 5th Beatle in the swinging sixties. I believe the young top players who have come through since have benefitted from George's experience in that they are protected from the media and live in secluded estates rather than being accessible to all the temptations that are everywhere for a superstar.

George packed an incredible amount into a relatively short, but outstanding career. He is there alongside the very greatest names in world football such as Pelé, Maradona, and Cruyff. There was always a lot of talk about an all-Ireland team and it would have been wonderful to have played International football alongside the likes of Jennings, Dougan and of course, the BEST of them all, George.

George Best Annual 1968

Eugene O'Hara

As a seven-year-old child I sat transfixed to the pictures on TV on 29 May 1968 to watch 'Georgie' Best. 'Georgie' Best made me the Man Utd fan which I have been ever since. Not sure how many children have heroes today, but I did and still do. Even today forty plus years and after all his difficulties George Best remains my boyhood hero.

I can't ever see that changing.

Sir Michael Parkinson

George often stayed with us when the media was looking for him. Our kids loved it. One day Michael, my youngest son, then six or seven was asked at school what he did at the weekend. He said 'Please miss, I played football with George Best'

He was made to stand in the corner for telling fibs!

Sir Michael and George in their cricket whites

We all have wonderful memories of George. I remember the first time I met him. I also remember the last time, which was actually in my pub shortly before he died. It was a reunion evening of Manchester United players of George's team. It was a lovely memory to take with me after George had died. It was an everlasting reminder of the pleasure he gave to all of us throughout the years. George wasn't just a great footballer, but a great star. He was a mini series waiting to be written.

CHRIS ARIF

John Beverley

I was eight years old (1968) and I cried the day my mother failed to get me a pair of George Best slippers out of the Grattan's catalogue. They were out of stock. What a surprise! Every time I played football at school, I was always 'Georgie' Best. I was and always will be besotted by the unbelievable skill of the 'Irish Wizard'.

I wish I could have met George and thanked him for my childhood memories.

Brendan, Armagh City

I'm a Gaelic fan from Armagh City, though supporting Manchester United from the mid-1950s comes a close second. I was born in 1946, just a few months before George, admired him and regarded him as a footballing genius from the first time I saw him play in Windsor Park, during my college days in the mid-1960s. George played at a time when pitches were far from the billiard-like surfaces we see today and tackles were frequently bone crushing, with little protection from match officials. Yet he rose above all this through his sheer skill and brilliance.

He was a supreme entertainer who made the pulses race every time he gained possession and he was the player who made the modern Manchester United. What a pity he never had the opportunity to play on the world stage, but still the sporting world knew all about him and mourns his passing.

You were the Best and we may never see your like again. Rest in Peace.

Harry Gregg Manchester United and Northern Ireland

George Best was one of the most gifted players in the history of football. It's not about me and my age, but I've been around for a long time and played with and against some of the greatest players in the game. Pelé, Garrincha, Beckenbaur, George is up there with them. George was a bright and shining star that was to burn out too quickly. The word 'hero' is overused, but in the case of George is very apt. George was a genius on the pitch. It was his domain. It is my personal belief that it was off the pitch where his coping mechanism failed him.

Martin, Bexleyheath, North London

I was born and brought up in London, am forty-three years old, and have you to blame George for thirty odd years as a Manchester United fan. Well George, you are the reason I am and always will be. I idolised you as a boy and as a man. God bless you, I never met you but will sorely miss you.

I loved to watch you play football
a lifelong MAN UTD FAN — Rest in Peace.

Birdie Got your Autograph in Manchester many
years ago, Thought you were brilliant!!!

Kaes
(manchester)

To a legend. The Best
manchester united player. x.

You introduced me to MUFC. I thank you forever
for the past 30yrs of pleasure. You are the BEST!

Mark The Reds could have done with you last night Bestie
Sorry I never had the chance to see you play
Hope your in a better place now — The 'Best' Always

Shane You are an Idol for all United fans RIP xo

Seán
+
Sarah

MARADONNA — GOOD
PELE — BETTER
GEORGE — BEST

M.U.F.C

Thanx 4 The Memories

I always felt like an entertainer and I loved to try things to get the crowd excited. To me it was just pure theatre.

BELFAST TELEGRAPH 20 OCTOBER 1973

He was such a special player, a phenomenal player and I think I speak for everyone at Manchester United when I say he left us with a million memories.

Sir Alex Ferguson

George Best was the most complete player the world has ever seen. He could tackle, head the ball and shoot. He had pace, he made goals and he scored them.

Sammy McIlroy. Manchester United and Northern Ireland

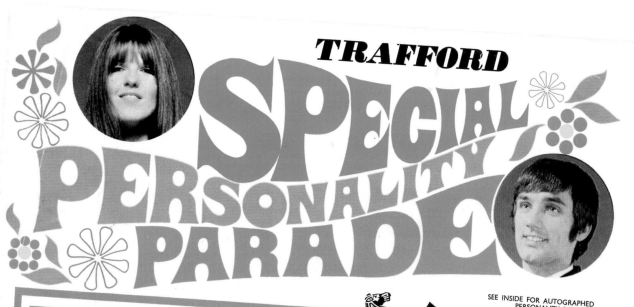

TRAFFORD
SPECIAL PERSONALITY PARADE

SEE INSIDE FOR AUTOGRAPHED PERSONALITY PICTURES

STYLO Matchmakers

GEORGE BEST

- Revolutionary side lacing. Tests prove that this shoe gives 25% more support.
- Made on a brand new exclusive last with a low line toeshape.
- Triple tone leather uppers.

- Best ball control. Perfectly smooth vamp.
- Special soles designed for greater flexibility, lightness and wear.

[A]

● Interchangeable and Multi Stud models.

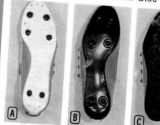

Left to Right

- Polyurethane Sole. Interchangeable Studs.

- Rubber Sole Interchangeable Studs.

- Rubber Sole. Moulded Studs.

[A]   [B]   [C]

The George Best Matchmaker by Stylo designed after many months, research. Good looks team with first class design to make this the Soccer shoe of the century — the Best! As comfortable as slippers, as strong as climbing boots — yet as light and streamlined as a track shoe. Builds confidence, improves the game.

Sizes: 6, 6½, 7, 7½, 8, 8½, 9, 9½, 10, 11

[A] Super Softie uppers, Polyurethane sole, interchangeable studs.
1P.5026C   Boots . . . . £7/7/0 . . . . 20 wks @ 7/4

[B] Rubber sole, interchangeable studs.
1P.5025F   Boots . . . . £5/5/0 . . . . 20 wks @ 5/3

[C] Standard model, Rubber sole moulded studs.
1P.5024M   Boots . . . . 95/11 . . . . 20 wks @ 4/10

[C] Boy's boot, as 1P.5024M;   Sizes: 2, 3, 4, 5
1P.2380E   Boots . . . . 65/11 . . . . 20 wks @ 3/4

A true 'Red Devil!'

George,
    I went to study in Manchester in the early '70s simply because you were there.
    I remember especially your goal against Sheffield United (when they were top of the league) which won the match.
    As a headteacher, many of the boys ask me who's my favourite player — they think I'm going to say someone playing now, but I never do — I always say — "George Best".

George —

GET WELL SOON !

Very best wishes,

Ed Daley.

Dorothy   I watched you play at Old Trafford you were magical — A legend!

LEGEND

7

Aidan   Robson, Cantona + Beckham My no. 7 legends, but you were Best !

George you were a wonderful footballer and person, I have been a fan since 1968

Heather   "Gentleman in Red"

THANK YOU FOR TEN YEARS OF pUER GEBNIUS ENTERTAINMENT GOD BLESS ALL THE R.I.P. GEORGE! BEST A MANCHESTER UNITED FAN

Anthony
Stretford End   Season Ticket Holder

Inspired me to support Man United, the best ever, never will be forgotten. Red Army.

SAM
TOBERMORE   A GENIUS.
FEELS LIKE I HAVE LOST A BROTHER.
God Bless.

Love
Maureen   Once a "God" playing with the Devils
Now a "God" playing with the Angels

Watched you Play As A little Girl with my Dad.

MANCHESTER UNITED

WWW.MANUTD.COM

Crest ©1997 MU PLC, © 2003 MUML

Love You George You were the Best
R.I.P. + Besley – Royton Oldham
+ DAD

100 YEARS FROM NOW WHEN THE CROWDS GATHER AT THE THEATRE OF DREAMS SOMEWHERE IN THE CROWD THEY'LL WHISPER 'GEORGE WAS THE BEST.

LEIGH   MAN UTD THRU + THRU
A GENIUS

You united my family with a common admiration for your artistry. Rest in Peace Did you know how loved you were

James   Never again will the hallowed turf of old Trafford ever be graced by a player of such original brilliance. The world of Football will weep, Never seeing the likes again. God bless it was a pleasure.

Andrew, High Wycombe

A shiver went down my spine when I finally heard the news that we had all been waiting for. I feel empty today. I'm twenty-seven and an Everton fan and Wayne Rooney was my hero. George Best was my father's who is a Manchester United fan. My father, a man of few words is even quieter than normal this evening. Today is a very sad day for everyone who loves football. I play for my local village side; I don't know if we will have a minute's silence tomorrow before our game. I'd like to think we will because I believe that football lovers and players no matter what level should take the time to reflect on the man that was George Best, a true genius.

Michael, Armagh

As a G.A.A. man and a Manchester United fan, I must say that Georgie, the Belfast Boy, was the greatest genius ever to grace a football pitch. May the angels bring you into paradise.

Dermot, Manchester

My dad was born in Northern Ireland in 1947, and came to Manchester I am sure in part, due to Georgie Best. He is a Manchester United fan and in turn so am I. I have had some of my Best memories because of football and I want to thank Georgie for this. My four-month-old daughter will be a Manchester United fan. This is the type of legacy George has left behind.

Thank you and rest in peace.

Who says they don't let (red) devils into heaven.

GEORGE - THANKYOU FOR YOUR LIFE

In Affectionate Remembrance

FOR MY FIRST HERO -
THE REASON I HAVE BEEN COMING
HERE FOR NEARLY FORTY YEARS.
FOR YOUR GRACE AND SPIRIT
YOU WILL BE REMEMBERED ALWAYS
SIMPLY, THE GREATEST PLAYER THE
WORLD HAS EVER SEEN. CHARLIE.

Paul, Wrotham, Kent

I shed a tear for you George, simply the Best. The most talented footballer and most loveable person that ever walked the earth. We will keep the red flag flying high. Rest in peace.

MANY HAVE WORN IT
BEFORE MANY. HAVE
WORN IT SINCE, BUT
THERE WILL ONLY BE
'ONE' MAGNIFICENT
7

THE 'BEST' THEIR'S
EVER BEEN · R.I.P

THE ABRAM FAMILY

YOU WERE THE BEST + AS
ONE RED 2 ANTOTHER ALWAYS WILL BE.

George may have Been MAN UTD'S Nº
7 - you are our Nº 1 - Ann + Dickie
Be Proud + Thanks for your son.

I never seen you live (Too young)
but you are one of the reasons
why I'm a Red!

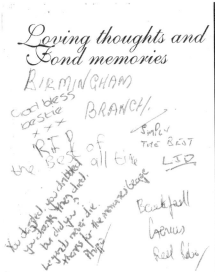

Loving thoughts and Fond memories

BIRMINGHAM
God bless
bestie   BRANCH/
x x x
R.I.P   SIMPLY
the Best of   THE BEST
            all time   LJD

Beckfield
Caprius
Red Rds/

MUCKAMORE REDS   We all live in a Georgie Best world.
M.U.S.C
ANTRIM

TO GEORGE

SETTING NOSTALGA ASIDE.
YOU ARE WITHOUT BOUBT, THE MOST
GIFTED AND NATURAL FOOTBALLER THE
WORLD AS EVER SEEN.
I WOULD LIKE TO THANK YOU, ON BEHALF
OF MY LATE DAO WALTER AND MY FRIEND
JOHNNY WILLIAMS. FOR ALL THE PLEASURE.
EXCITEMENT, AND WONDERFUL MEMORIES, WE
SHARED TOGETHER.

ALL THE GEORGIE

JOHN McCARTHY.

Martin, Bradbury

He was born in the back streets of Belfast. Some say he was born too soon, for if he had been born today he would have known no gloom. He stood only 5 feet 8 inches and weighed only 9 stones. By day he played with his friends, by night he played on his own. Then early one morning a letter arrived at his home saying 'will your son take the ferry from Ireland to England alone'.

So a young man arrived at Old Trafford prepared to give it his all, but Ireland is a long way from England and the Emerald Isle they'd call. It took all Matt Busby's persuading to make him come back for a test but he knew he'd found a genius who was so far ahead of the rest. He could run like a greyhound and turn on a sixpence to shoot. He could dribble his way through a minefield while still only wearing one boot. The crowds they all flocked in their thousands, his antics attacked by the press, but they all had to bow down to true genius, George Best!

Rest in peace, we will all miss you.

Cameron I think you were one of the best Players in the world. Thank you for leading Man Utd to glory.

TRUE RED

EL BEATLE

Dustin, Northfleet

Football has lost one of its greatest if not the greatest player ever. It is fitting that United's next Euro game is against Benfica, who Bestie terrorised in that famous quarter-final, and United's next home game is against West Bromwich, who George made his Manchester United debut against.

To the United of today, please make sure you play in the memory of El Beatle in those two games. God bless you George and thank you for the memories.

5th BEATLE

A FAN OF THE "FIFTH"
BEATLE XX

Sure we had problems with the wee fella, but I prefer to remember his genius.

He was able to use either foot. Sometimes he seemed to have six!

Let him alone. Don't try to coach him. The boy is special.

MATT YOUR BABE HAS RETURNED

CANTWELL BUSBY, AND NOW BEST. WHAT A TEAM UP ABOVE.

Sir Matt + george Best = A great United Squad.

WHAT A TEAM HEAVEN HOLDS NOW SIR MATT THE BUSBY BABES + NOW ONE TRUE LEGEND GEORDIE BEST AND HE WAS'NT FROM BRAZIL BUT NORN IRON. R.I.P

. Keep the Red flag flying high Man united will never die. Rest in peace our greastest ever player. with Sir Matt busby again

YOU DONE FOR MATT BUSBY & MAN U WHAT HENRIK LARRSON DONE FOR MARTIN O NEILL & CELTIC.
Joe

Best your simply the Best your now with God Matt Busby and will look after you God Bless Best!

(Father) & Son once more re-UNITED
(Sir matt) (George)

FOR ALL THE GOALS THANKS. SAY HELLO TO SIR MATT, HE'LL SEE YOU RIGHT. YOU'RE MISSED

Replica programme from George's debut match

JOHN MANCHESTER
George = you gave me & my family a million thrills as we watched you with LAW + CHARLTON every match at old Trafford in the 60's God Bless John d

Samantha
Simply the Best ⑦
You were the greatest player to ever wear a Man.Utd shirt. You were an amazing player. Thanks for all the skills, goals + incredible memories. You will be sadly missed. God Bless you. xx

Paul, Welshpool

George Best was my childhood hero and I am very upset. I asked my grandfather whom he played for when I was about 5 years old; from then on I was a Manchester United fan. I wish I could have met him and put an arm around him, because I feel I did know him. He was the Best.

They kicked lumps out of him on the field and he always got up. Just think what he would do now given the rules on tackling. Thanks for the great memories George. You will always live on in the hearts of football fans. My deepest sympathy George's family, you should be proud of the joy he gave me and millions of others.

Sublime, Brilliant. You wee & are the Greatest footballer NO7 to wear a Manu Shirt. Rest in Peace. You Torment nouce! x

'Dear George, thanks for the memories. You were the Mozart of football, love Elton John'

Johnny ONE MAN IS NO BIGGER THAN THE CLUB BUT MAN UTD WOULD HAVE BEEN A LESSER CLUB TODAY IF YOU NEVER PLAYED FOR THEM. GOOD LUCK GEORGIE!!

Mike, Kent

As a kid growing up in a hard working environment with little money, watching George play and reading about him, without a doubt brightened my day. I loved and admired everything about his game. I never met him yet felt that I knew him. Whenever I used to hear anything bad said against him I had to defend him. Watching the footage yesterday of George at his Best brought it home to me why I fell in love with football, and Manchester United. It was solely down to George. How many other people or experiences make the hairs stand up on the back of your neck, make you shiver, laugh, cry and nearly all at the same time? I felt that something is missing in my life since yesterday because there won't be any more news about what he has been up to.

Thanks for the happy memories.

I would like to thank you and your family for allowing me as a member of the public and a huge George Best fan the honour of attending the Memorial Service held in Manchester Cathedral on 16th March. The day was one which I will never forget. George was and always will be my hero. I grew up in Belfast and moved to England in 1964 and have been a Manchester United fan since 1963. I go to watch United whenever I can and the reason I support them is down to George.

Colin

TAGS MANCHESTER You LIVED THE DREAM, WE LIVED IT THROUGH YOU. I'm A UNITED FAN BECAUSE OF YOU, TAGS

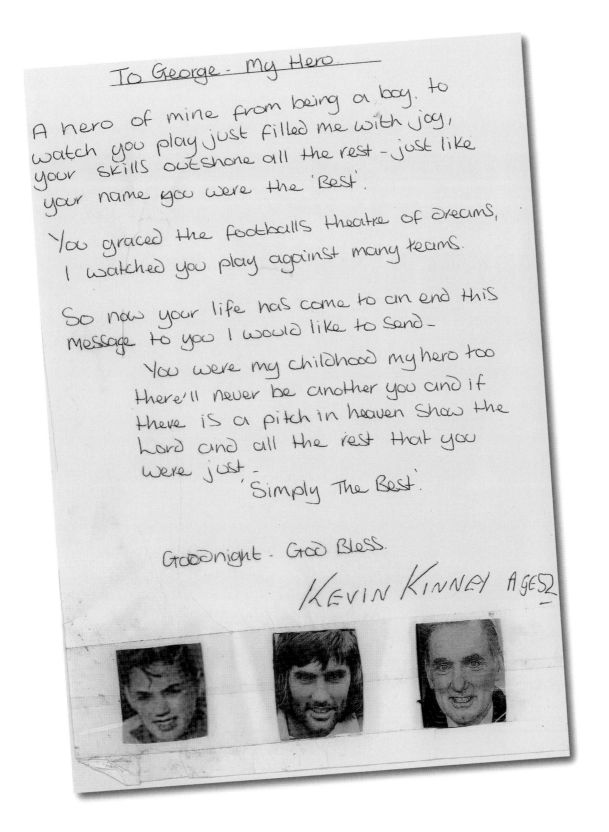

To George - My Hero

A hero of mine from being a boy. to
watch you play just filled me with joy,
your skills outshone all the rest - just like
your name you were the 'Best'.

You graced the football's theatre of dreams,
I watched you play against many teams.

So now your life has come to an end this
message to you I would like to send -

You were my childhood my hero too
there'll never be another you and if
there is a pitch in heaven show the
Lord and all the rest that you
were just -
'Simply The Best'.

Goodnight - God Bless.

KEVIN KINNEY AGE 52

Sven Goran Eriksson

His ability was an inspiration to everyone who loves football.
He was known around the world for his skill and flair.

Angela   Rest in peace, and at last have no pain.
Manchester.

TOMMY
ASHTON-U-LYNE MANCHESTER

THANKS GEORGEY YOU BROUGHT ME LOTS
OF PLEASURE WHEN I WAS WAS A BOY. I STILL
WORSHIP YOU NOW 40 YEARS LATER R.I.P.

STEVE
MANCHESTER
MANCHESTER.

SIMPLE THE BEST EVER R.I.P.

GOD BLESS YOU GEORGIE R.I.P.

TERRY

BEST FOOTBALLER EVER! LEGEND!

From the Committe and members
Manchester United Supporters Club
Ireland Branch Founded 1969

From all the Manchester United Fan from the Isle of Man
"WE ALWAYS MISS YOU" LEGEND FOREVER.
COLIN

DENIS LAW WAS THE KING OF "OLD TRAFFORD
BUT GEORGE WAS THE GOD!

SIMPLY THE GREATEST
UNITED IN LIFE UNITED IN DEATH

One of Man.U's greatest players
EL BEATLE ADIOS ME AMIGO.

And they chanted, "we don't need Eusabio 'cos we've got Georgie

OLD TRAFFORD HAS ALWAYS BEEN A THEATRE.
GEORGE YOU MADE IT THE "THEATRE OF DREAMS"
GOD BLESS   COLIN

Ded   Man U Fan — Best ever. Thanks George.
     1957 →

Billy   I HAD THE PRIVLAGE OF SEEING YOU PLAY
         AT OLD TRAFORD & IN GERMANY. YOU WHERE FANTASTIC
                                       WILL NEVER FORGET YOU.
Séan   YOU WERE SIMPLY A GENIUS,
         AND YOU WILL BE SORELY MISSED.   M·U·F·C forever

Jesse, Galway

I am a Manchester United fan who was born in Galway in 1975. I never saw George play live and as a young boy, I used to watch Maradona and was mesmerised. My Dad, who was a huge fan of George and once played a Sunday morning kick around with him in 1964, bought me a video when I was about six or seven. That was the first time I saw George and to this day and without any doubt I consider him to be the most outrageously brilliant football player I ever had the good fortune to see. Maradona had to take a back seat!

We all know of George's indiscretions and which of us has none? For me, George was, is and always will be a class act. For someone I've never met, to have had such an effect on me is strange but at the same time nice.

I would just simply like to thank him for making what can be sometimes a dull world, that little bit brighter.

George

Sadly I never saw you play. except on tv clips but you are and always will be a legend. as a Man U fan I am proud you played for the best club in the world. All the best above with Sir Matt and all the greats.

Ronán

Tributes left by fans at Old Trafford

GOD BLESS FROM A STOCKPORT RED - PURE GENIUS REST IN PEACE x.

IN RED OR GREEN HE WAS SUPREME THE BEST.

WARRENPOINT MANCHESTER UNITED SUPPORTERS CLUB SIMPLY THE BEST - AN UNDER STATEMENT!

George Best the great player, I saw Him with great Hat trick for Man U against West Ham in 1971, with saddness, Anthony Man United fan

ALL THE Best Big Man you were the life and soul of our team the red Devils and always will be !!!

(7)-(11) COMPLETE LEGENDS

"UTD" SHOULD HAVE WRAPPED YOU IN COTTON WOOL. THEY DIDN'T APPRECIATE WAAT THEY HAD A "GENIUS."

Robertson Davies

George, he was a genius. That is to say, a man who does superlatively well and without obvious effort, something that most people cannot do, even by the uttermost exertion of their abilities.

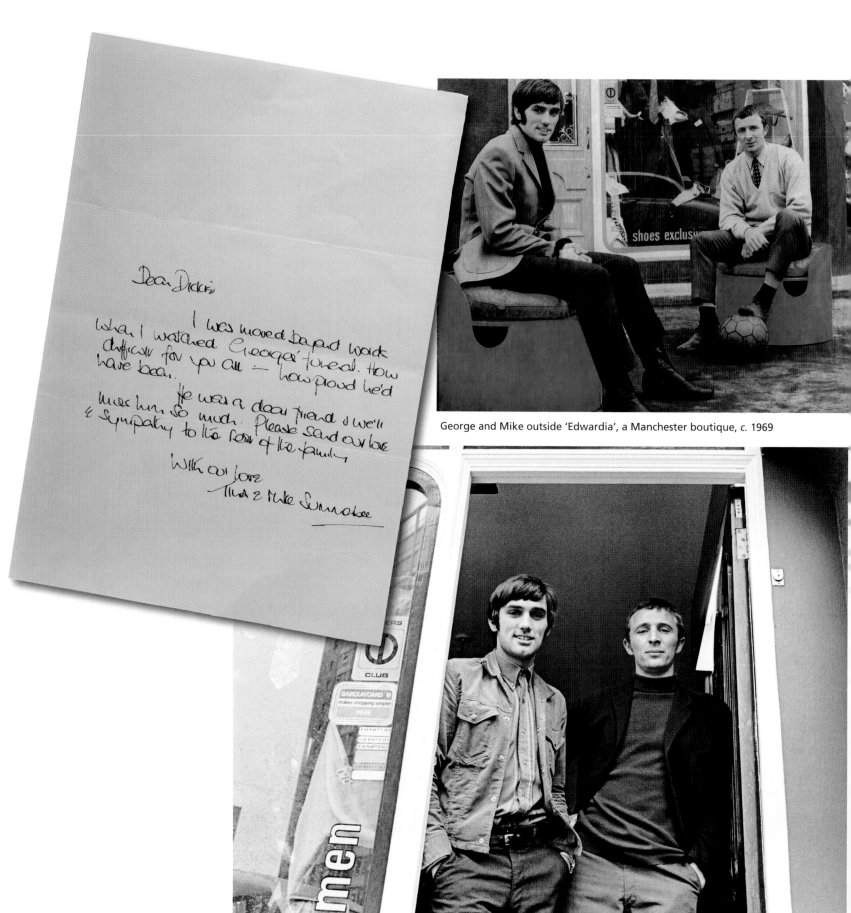

Dear Dickie

I was moved beyond words
when I watched George's funeral. How
difficult for you all — how proud he'd
have been.

He was a dear friend & we'll
miss him so much. Please send our love
& sympathy to the rest of the family

With our love
Tina & Mike Summerbee

George and Mike outside 'Edwardia', a Manchester boutique, c. 1969

BONHAMS AUCTION

Football Writers' Player of the Year,
1968

A MAN UNITED WITH HIS MUM

Nº 7 FOOTBALL SHIRT
Nº 1 FOOTBALL LEGEND

PLAYED FOR UNITED, UNITED THE PEOPLE, GOD BLESS

Best was the best player in the whole of Man Utd Faster than an eagle, And it even says what he was in his name the BEST! but now it's time to say goodbye, We all love you Best!!! Connor

George Best ... aptly named. So glad you wore the red of Utd.

Belfasts own legend. I know you'll be looking down @ Old Trafford. R.I.P "Georgie Boy"

Brian

The time was the mid-sixties. I was seven-years-old and listened to my grandfather marvel at the ability of this lad called Best. Because of this, because of George, like so many others before and since, I began to support Manchester United. I watched enthralled as he made great players and in those days they were GREAT, look foolish. He turned hard men to jelly. What would George be worth today? In an era of bowling green pitches, defenders allowed to make no sort of physical contact etc., etc. My own son, who is twenty, is too young to have seen George playing, but recently has watched videos and now himself marvels at George's ability.

Discussions will go on as to how to have George Best remembered. Individuals will have their own memories that can never be taken away. I certainly have mine. He was the finest footballer I have ever seen and a true entertainer.

GEORGE BEST
(Manchester United and N. Ireland)

George Best joined Manchester United in May 1963 and is now one of the world's most famous footballers. With 13 full caps to his credit so far he has often played a decisive role in many important matches. After his third place in the 1966 'Footballer of the Year' Award he won the award in 1968. His versatile and individual style of play has now put him in the front rank of 'all-time greats' in the game.

David Beckham   Manchester United and England

I always saw George as a football legend and it was a proud moment when I wore the same number 7 jersey as him. He was the greatest player to have ever graced the game.

David, Gosfield

In 1968, you were the first ever picture on my wall with a Typhoo tea picture. Stylo Matchmaker boots and slippers followed, shirt [hanging] out, but hell I could never grow sideburns. You were my first and longest lasting hero and I would like to thank you for the smiles and joy that you have brought me.

Northern Ireland versus England, Windsor Park, Belfast, 1966

NORTHERN IRELAND DAYS

George first pulled on the famous green jersey of Northern Ireland on 15 April 1964, to play in their Home International 3–2 victory against Wales in Swansea. He was just seventeen years-old and extremely proud that his country had selected him. It was some achievement given that only seven short months earlier he'd made his first team debut for Manchester United. There is little doubt that George's association with Manchester United is still one of the main reasons why support for them in Northern Ireland is absolutely huge today.

Then, George was at the start of a phenomenal football career, a career which would catapult him to international fame and worldwide recognition. Despite this, sadly George never competed in a World Cup competition, but this never stopped him from making the headlines.

Today, statistics blandly tell us that George went on to play thirty-seven times for his country, scoring nine goals, which included a hat-trick against Cyprus at Windsor Park in 1971. Statistics however, are incapable of conveying the excitement and passion which George brought to every single Northern Ireland game and fan who watched him play.

This section includes messages which were drawn from books of condolence, letters, cards, poems and emails sent to Ulster Television and talkSPORT at the time of George's death.

Northern Ireland

Meet me in Belfast   David Brailsford

Meet me in Belfast
At George Best Airport
We'll say goodbye
To the Belfast boy
Mourn the past
Embrace the future
Tears of loss
With tears of joy

Meet me in Belfast
And be beside me
Give me strength
To kneel and pray
Giving thanks
For George's life
And for the love
We feel this day

Meet me in Belfast
The chosen city
Birthplace of
A football dream
Sublime, unique
And at his peak
The greatest player
There's ever been

PAT JENNINGS   Tottenham Hotspur and Northern Ireland

George Best was unquestionably the most complete player I ever saw. A talent beyond compare. He possessed all the technical attributes, was blessed with good looks, charisma and an hypnotic appeal. He was the first of the superstars of football.

You could not have wished for a more loyal team mate and I should know as we shared rooms from our first meeting in April 1964 when we were both selected by Northern Ireland for the British Championship game against Wales at the Vetch Field Swansea. I was eighteen and a Third Division player at Watford. George was a year younger.

George had two reputations during his football career – one for his skill on the field, the other for his peccadilloes and exploits off it and celebrity lifestyle. I admit I only know one of them. The footballer who left a wonderful legacy, a fulfilment of his boyhood dreams. It is a pity that his International (just thirty-seven caps) and his club reigns ended so prematurely as did his life with him passing away at a comparatively young age.

We struck up a friendship from that day in Swansea where we defeated Wales 3–2 and a fortnight later the same team triumphed 3–0 over Uruguay at Windsor Park, a stadium with a wonderful tradition and heritage generating an atmosphere unsurpassed at Internationals. Windsor Park was Northern Ireland's twelfth man.

It was there in 1967 that George produced one of the most spectacular and scintillating displays virtually on his own against Scotland. George was a genius, a quality player who arrives on the scene once in a lifetime revealing a bewildering repertoire of swerves, feints, elasticity of limb, deceptive change of pace, astonishing physical strength and the ability to 'ride' the fiercest tackles despite his small frame which carried not an ounce of fat.

The fans idolised him. His El Beatle hairstyle, those twinkling blue eyes, fantastic sense of humour and film star good looks attracted like a magnet the glamour women of the world.

He had nerves of steel. Even before major matches, he would sit in a corner of the dressing room, reading the paper or pondering over *The Times* crossword

To George Best with love from
Alex Higgins. With deepest
sympathy to the Best family

puzzle which he could complete in record time. He was articulate, a voracious
reader and could discuss many subjects other than football.

Northern Ireland has never remotely had a better player than George and his
biggest regret was that he never played in a World Cup finals series, which would
have been an ideal platform to parade his skills.

The warmth and memories which I have of George are felt by many, particularly
in Northern Ireland as was evident by the interest and attendance at his funeral
from Parliament Buildings at Stormont. A unique day in the Province's history.

George's name will live forever in the annals of football as the boy from Burren
Way in east Belfast who became an iconic figure bringing artistry and enjoyment
to millions as did his friends, Pelé, Maradona and Cruyff.

I doubt we will ever see his like again.

Pat Fenning

Pat signs his autograph at the George Best Golf Invitational
at Galgorm Castle Golf Club, 2008

belfast boy

Eamonn Holmes TV Presenter

Birthdays are supposed to be happy and memorable times. My 46th one is one that I will never forget. On Saturday 3rd December 2005 I was centre stage for all the wrong reasons, but I was honoured to be there. George's family had asked me to host his homecoming. Unfortunately it was to be his last return to Belfast – because this was his funeral. The weather was absolutely foul. It was very cold with rain coming down like stair rods, making everywhere dank and depressing. But still people turned out. Not just in their thousands or tens of thousands but in hundreds of thousands. They knew none of us would ever see his like again. He had put us on the map, he had made us feel important. George Best had made wee Norn Ireland very, very big. We were all very sad but we were all very proud too – so proud we didn't even feel the rain.

A family grieved, football grieved and a country grieved as well. In Ulster folklore we have many heroes, many legends and many myths. George Best will pass into that folklore as mercurial, as magical, as someone who lived his dream and as someone who made our dreams come true. What mere mortal could do what he did on a pitch? George would always recognise, that however much of a genius he may have been, he was also flawed and maybe that imperfection made us love him more.

In a country that often couldn't rise above politics and religion, George Best did more than most to bring us together as a people, to make us realise that there is more to unite us than to divide us. George, we mourned your life cut short but we were proud to welcome you home to Northern Ireland as your final resting place.

If there are regrets around George's life, it may be because many of us, like him had an addiction. We were greedy for more and more was never going to be enough. I regret I didn't see him play more often. I regret as a child I didn't realise just how good he was. I regret that television technology in his day was not multi-camera and recorded in HD. But more than that I rejoice that as such a small country, Northern Ireland had for a short time the most famous and talented footballer in the world.

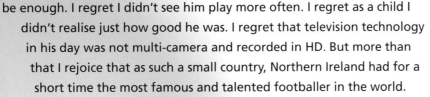

Eddie Irvine Formula 1 racing driver

For me, George was one of those special people whose talent and love of life made a lasting impression on a whole generation. A Belfast Boy, a footballer by profession, a player both on and off the field, he was a hero of our times. A legend, he will never be forgotten.

'One o The Lads'

My memories of a footballer that mesmerised you from the moment he touched the ball, to anticipation of what he was going to do next, it left you breathless. To me, he was the most exciting player the world has ever seen, or will ever see again.

What made him special to me?

He was no different to any of us, he was just 'One o the Lads'

From Manchester to Marbella, everyone knew him and all can tell a story. They are precious memories, which not even the press can destroy.

You were and still are in the hearts and souls of all who had the pleasure to meet you. I am one of those people that remember you for what you are George.

'One o the Lads'

In action for Northern Ireland 1967

George versus Gordon Banks for the goal that never was

Trevor Ringland MBE   Ulster, Ireland, and British and Irish Lions Rugby player

I was there on the day when George scored that 'goal' when Northern Ireland played England. In true George Best style he cheekily kicked the ball out of the great Gordon Banks' hands and then put the ball into the goal. As we all know, it was disallowed, but to all who were there or saw it on TV, it will always be a goal of character.

When growing up we all wanted to be George Best or if our footballing skills were not up to it, then, those such as me, always had Pat Jennings to try and emulate. What two great ambassadors from our small part of the world and who best reflect the rich talent of friendship that the people here have and is their true character.

Magic moments never to be forgotten.

An inspiration & hope. The kadds Shining Star, Ulstars prayers answered. An icon, a genius, and a gentleman. The Greatest sportsman to grace the world stage. Our son, our hero, our legend. Mortally blessed, heavenly rest. Forever.X

FOOTBALLS VAN GOGH
THANKS FOR THE "BEST" MEMORIES

I'LL NEVER FORGET MEETING GEORGE BEST
IN PERSON, HIS GENUINE WARMTH CAME
ACROSS SO STRONGLY, A FANTASTIC PERSON ON &
OFF THE FOOTBALL PITCH. GOD BLESS YOU. R.I.P

To the Belfast Boy who never grew up, you were a godsend to N. Ireland, you had the heart, the Soul and most of all the touch of magic. God Bless you george! xxx

You WERE A PURE LEGEND. Thank you for the memories, you were probably the only thing that all people of NI could agree on. Forever in our hearts, George. XX.

Comparing you to today's players is like comparing a Porsche to a tractor – the tractor will get you there in the end but the Porsche will do it with style!

PRESS EYE, BELFAST

HUGH McILVANNEY   Sports journalist

His game was an amalgam of superb, almost unnatural balance, spirit and delicacy of touch that stayed no matter how fast he moved. Mesmerising deft feet with an acrobatic balance, unlimited inventiveness and nerveless insouciance.

BARRY DAVIES   Sports commentator

More words have been written and spoken about George than about any other sportsman. Few have done justice to his talents.

There was an unfettered joy about the way he played. He combined grace with courage, pace with unbelievable balance, He was balletic and yet at the same time aggressive. Warming to the heart and yet clinically cold in his application. He was the master of the unexpected. The most gifted of Saturday's heroes and the most tormented.

£5
GEORGE BEST
1946 - 2005
George Best
BEST
£5
✳✳Ulster Bank Limited

In the books of history your name will remain
The greatest footballer was from Belfast and
George Best was his name

George with Tobermore United, 1984

Irene
TOBERMORE
+
Sara-Louise

WILL ALWAY'S REMEMBER THE DAY
YOU PLAYED FOR TOBERMORE UNITED.
GOD BLESS.

Tobermore
The Boot.

Patrick Kielty Comedian

It makes you proud to say that you are from Northern Ireland. For years when I first started up in London, there was the notion that if you came from the south of Ireland, you had this lilting accent, carried a copy of Joyce's *Ulysses* under your arm and had a pint of Guinness in your hand. They were the story tellers, whilst in Northern Ireland, we were considered to be the ones who wore balaclavas and told you that you had five minutes to get out.

One of the small diamonds in the dirt was George Best and as time went on, you realised that you could hold your head high.

Good bye to a legend.

you are in a better place now

you were some footballer

Final whistle has been blown but the game ain't over.
God bless.

Brendan, Reading

Dear George, I never had the chance to meet you however because of you I won many arguments as a budding young footballer. I left Northern Ireland to join Reading FC at fifteen and was always asked to name a player from Northern Ireland who was any good! Immediately I would always reply 'George Best'. At this point, no-one said anything, and then I would ask them to name me a player better than George Best, they never could.

I only hoped that in my current job as Youth Team Coach at Chelsea FC our paths would cross but at five minutes to one o'clock today I knew they never would. I can now only pay tribute to someone who made me proud to be from Northern Ireland and heaven will be a better place with you in it.

Rest in peace from a Carnlough man.

CHRIS

TO AN AWESOME LOCAL PLAYER,
TO A NATIONAL HERO,
TO A WORLDWIDE LEGEND! IRREPLACABLE AND NEVER FORGOTTEN!

It is an honour to honour the memory of Northern Ireland's *Best*
Alderman William DeCourcy. Mayor. N.B. Council

Ald. I. Robinson MP   Remembered for your talent on
the pitch. Every sympathy for
the Best family! May God richly
bless you in your time
of mourning.

Councillor Jim Rodgers   Fondly Remembered. It was a pleasure to have known
you.
God Bless.

Queen's Graduates' Association

5th December 2005

Dear Mr Best,

On behalf of the Queen's Graduates Association I should
like to send our condolences to you and all the family circle.

In December 2001 George received his honorary degree of
Doctor of the University and part of the citation read "The
University honours one of our own, a Belfast Boy, who made
an historic and unsurpassed contribution to Association
Football, rightly described as "the beautiful game", and who
did so with a unique blend of skill and glamour".

We were very proud of our honorary graduate and sorry to
lose him so soon.

I know that large numbers of graduates would like to have
been at the funeral on Saturday and many lined the route in
respect, so I felt very privileged to have been able to attend
on their behalf. It was an extremely moving service and I am
sure you were very proud of your daughter and grandson
who spoke so well.

You will all be in our thoughts and prayers in the weeks
ahead and I hope that the knowledge that so many people
are with you will help to ease your sorrow at this time.

Yours sincerely

Patricia Shates (Mrs)

President QGA

QUEEN'S UNIVERSITY
BELFAST
CLASS '01
THURSDAY 13TH DECEMBER 2001

The Freedom of the Borough of Castlereagh
presented to George on 3 April 2002

BONHAMS

Presented to
GEORGE BEST
On The Occasion Of The
FREEDOM OF THE BOROUGH OF CASTLEREAGH
3 April 2002

1964 - 1977

JOHN HARRISON PHOTOGRAPHY

THE WORLD HAS LOST IT'S GREATEST EVER PLAYER.
HIS LEGACY AND MANY HAPPY MEMORIES WILL NEVER BE ALLOWED
TO FADE!

I witnessed Best at Windsor Park and wondered.
if Burns, Bach or Rembrandt; King Billy, St Patrick
or Cuchulain got reincarnated as a footballer.

Chase Ruttenberg, Vancouver, with his George Best
No. 1 sticker

Titanic, Canberra, and George, A Belfast Hat-trick of Legends
With Sympathy

60's ICON - PERSONIFIED THE BRITISH GOLDEN
ERA — ALL THE WAY FROM NORTHERN IRELAND
WE LOVED YOU . XX

Well Support you ever more.
(FIRST LISBURN M.S.C)

GENIUS NEVER FORGOTTEN
(BRING HIM HOME). X.

Don Mullan

May 1971. My hero was Gordon Banks. I travelled from Derry to see Northern Ireland play England at Windsor Park in the old Home Internationals. But because of Banks, I was an Irishman with a dilemma. Wanting Northern Ireland to win against the ol' enemy but not wanting my hero to concede a goal.

And then came that moment of controversy, still remembered and debated, when a mischievous George Best pounced. Like magic, the ball suddenly disappeared somewhere between the iconic goalkeeper's hands and right boot. The fans saw George's sleight of hand, though in this case, his sleight of foot. Banks, momentarily baffled, realised too late what had been done, chasing and diving in vain as George headed the ball into the back of the England net and the home supporters went wild – except me!

If it had been Peter Shilton or any other England goalkeeper, it would have been a goal. No doubt about it. But Banksy? No way! How could I celebrate a goal against my hero? When the referee disallowed the goal, I had to contain myself, or face ducking a Windsor wallop.

Years later, the great Pat Jennings, who played opposite Banksy that day, told me that the following week at Old Trafford George did exactly the same thing to him. But on that occasion, the referee let the goal stand.

Such magical memories. Thank you George.

Cllr. Alex Maskey — With my very deepest sympathy to all George's loved one - family and friends.

The Big Ref has blown full time

United's No 7   Ulsters No 1

Life is a Patchwork
and Today you start a New Design — God Bless, George
x

Ian Paisley jnr M.L.A   The Best footballer the World has ever Seen.

ON BEHALF OF THE BOYS
1ST BATT. ROYAL IRISH CURRENTLY SERVING IN.
IRAQ. A TRUE LEGEND RIP.
DEEPEST SIMPATHY TO ALL.

MADE OUR LATE FATHER VERY HAPPY
TELLING US OF THE STORIES OF GEORGE
BEST EVER (GENTLEMAN)

YOU'LL BE SADLY MISSED BY HUNDREDS OF FANS ☺

LOWER SHANKILL N.I.S.C,   A LEGEND IN LIFE
                          A LEGEND IN DEATH GOD BLESS

HOWARD WELLS   IFA   A legend in real terms

Jim Boyce   PRESIDENT IFA   Someone who I respected as a true friend

NEIL
CHAIRMAN
1ST GLENTORAN N.I.S.C.   EAST BELFAST'S FINEST, YOU WILL BE TRULY MISSED BY
ALL FOOTBALL FANS IN BELFAST AND THE WORLD OVER.
THERE WAS NO ONE BETTER.

May your beautiful spirit surround us forever

Gary Callaghan

United had just won the Treble but my BEST dream was just about to come true!

From Barcelona to Carrickfergus in three days and the scene was set. I was the Secretary of the Carrickfergus MUSC and I had spent the season watching the Reds' every game. In between times, I was organising what was to become a great finale to our season. How was I to know United would win the treble and we would have three legends at our end of season function. Best, Law and Crerand?

Having known Paddy for many years I had asked him to help me get in touch with George and Denis. The scene had been set for 450 dinner places in total. Off I went to collect the Lawman, another hero of mine from the airport. Denis was checked in to the Hotel and given his customary pot of tea. Now to collect Paddy from the 'George Best' Belfast City Airport and on to pick George up at the International Airport. BMI flight BD88 from London had arrived but where was George? Oh no I thought! Paddy asked the girl at the desk if she could find out if George Best was in the airport and the call came back that George and Alex were having liquid refreshments in the bar! Paddy's words cannot be repeated but within five minutes Bestie was in the back seat of my car and on his way to Carrickfergus.

I was star struck. My rearview mirror confirmed that I was in the presence of my all time boyhood hero George Best. George chatted warmly on the twenty-five mile journey, he had the ability to make you feel that you had known him all your life. Perhaps I did, having been a fan of his from the age of seven or eight and the reason I, like so many others, are Manchester United supporters today.

George went to the bar for a glass of wine and I went to check on the function room ahead of the evening event. Seven-thirty arrived and so did 450 guests, but, Bestie was not to be found! A local taxi driver exclaimed that he had just seen George Best in the local filling station doing his lottery. Panic over. Fifteen minutes later Best, Law and Crerand took centre stage. A great night was to unfold especially for the kids from Whitehaven Respite Unit who came in for special and affectionate attention from George.

Sunday morning, following breakfast with my wife Marie and Alex, George said his dad was on his way and he wanted us to meet him. The hours that followed were when I truly realised what a lovely person George Best really was. He introduced me to his Dad as if I was the genius. I had just met another great man, Dickie Best, and how unassuming they both were. Having seen George play several times in real life, I found myself gazing at his eyes and then those magic feet. It was soon time to say goodbye and we all set off for the airport, oh how I didn't want that day to end. Hugs and kisses were exchanged. I never met George again.

For the pleasure George has given me all my life and for the weekend I had just spent in his company, I owed him! I have always been a fanatical Man Utd supporter and have met many great players, however no player will ever live in my heart the way George does. George, you were a genius. Thanks for the memories!

Sean

My favourite memory was going to
Windsor Park in 1977 when Northern
Ireland played Holland in a World Cup
qualifier. Georgie put the ball through
Johann Cruyff's legs with great aplomb.

Also when he scored against Gordon Banks
but the silly ref disallowed it. The chip over
Pat Jennings v Spurs.

Also fond memories of stylo boots; e-type
jags; nightclubs called Slack Alice and the
fun time at Fulham with Rodney Marsh and
Bobby Moore, etc.

God bless his family and may Georgie rest
in peace at last.

George in action against Gordon Banks. Northern Ireland versus England,
Windsor Park, 15 May 1971

*Tell Gordon Banks! ~ He knows it was
a GOAL!!!*

LIMAVADY UTD F.C.
    REMEMBERED ~ GOD BLESS
RECOVERD   GOD BLESS   GEORGE
    ALCOHLIC   SLEEP TIGHT · XXX

A HERO TO ALL REGARDLESS OF RACE, CREED OR COLOUR
A BEACON OF LIGHT THAT CROSSED ULSTER'S DIVISION
REST IN PEACE GEORGE AND GOD BLESS

Gordon Banks

Most Irish people like to remind me about the incident that happened at the international match in Belfast during the Home Internationals in 1971 involving George. I recall picking up a through ball near the six-yard line. George came running towards me, and stood quite close. I started to do what I would normally do. I bounced the ball forward then threw it up in the air to kick it long. George knew that I threw the ball fairly high so as it was coming down, he flicked the ball over my head. We both turned to try and get to the ball, but he managed to reach it first and headed it into the net! I didn't hear a whistle go, that's the reason I chased it, but the ref had blown for a free kick against George. I have always said that he didn't touch me at all. The reason the ref didn't give the goal was because if my foot was coming up to kick the ball, I could have broken my leg on his foot!

George was very fast. You may remember in those days we had a lot of slow centre forwards that wouldn't have been as quick as George . He had this wonderful aptitude of waiting until a defender was about to make a tackle. He'd know the guy was about to lunge and he'd push the ball, ride the tackle and off he'd fly towards the goal. Next the defender would try to bring him down because he couldn't afford to let George free and still he could ride the tackle and still stay on his feet while the defender is now on the floor, out of the game. He had the ability to carve a huge opening, get clear through and kill the defence. I've never seen a player able to do this as well as George could. It was absolutely fantastic.

He scored a goal at Stoke. I've got a frame of it at home – he had three of us going, two defenders and me with just the movement of his body. George was on the edge of the box and Willie Morgan, Manchester United's right winger, a slim lad, drove the ball across to him. He killed it stone dead and then pushed it forward on his right foot. Denis Smith was only a couple of yards away from him and, believe me, Denis would throw himself at anything. He would break a leg to stop a bloke from shooting. Denis threw himself at him. George stopped, pulled the ball around Denis with his right foot and left him stranded. Alan Bloor then came in to tackle him. George lifted the ball with his left foot – same thing. Alan goes to block it and suddenly George pulls it back round on his right foot. Alan is left stranded and George is now in the penalty spot position. There's nobody on him so I came off my line. He saw me coming, dummied me, throws me completely the wrong way, pulls the ball around me and rolls it over the blooming line. What a bloody goal! An absolutely magnificent goal it was – absolutely fantastic. And then the little sod says to me: 'Pick that out Banksy', laughing as he headed back up the field. He was a great player, terrific player, it's just a real shame he retired early in his career. He spoiled a lot of people's pleasure because he used to fill a ground. They literally would come to see George Best play. Then he became ill with alcoholism, which is so tragic. Many are sad that it worked out for him like it did.

George was one of the most truly talented and gifted players that I have ever had the privilege to play against in the whole of my footballing career. He was a smashing bloke.

Scotland at Windsor 1967 – unbelievable one man show!

NI. /1 Scotland 0 Thanks for the memories

Tommy Gemmell, Celtic and Scotland

comment following the Scotland match 21 October 1967

It's the only match which left me with the flu as I stood in a constant draught as George went past! He tore me apart. I couldn't even catch him to kick him. With respect to the other Irish lads, it was George Best against Scotland and he won. I played against the best in the world, but never faced another Best. He was pure genius and a lovely guy.

On 21 October 1967, George practically defeated Scotland on his own during a Saturday afternoon game played at Windsor Park. This game, which Northern Ireland eventually won 1–0, was later dubbed the 'George Best against Scotland game' and regarded by many leading sports critics of the day as being the greatest individual performance to be seen anywhere in the world at the time. This was the game when every single George Best body swerve, every George Best feigned pass, was cheered on passionately by every Northern Ireland fan.

Following the Scotland match, newspaper headlines the following Sunday morning recorded the irony of living a life in a 'troubled' Northern Ireland. Banner front page headlines in the morning papers focused on the violent and socially disturbing events, 'Barricades in the streets as a shooting war breaks out in Belfast' whilst below this depressing headline was a beautiful photograph of a smiling George with his family. In stark contrast, the back page banner headline recorded something far more positive, something which noted George's amazing bravura performance in the previous afternoon's game against Scotland, It simply read: 'Giant George Architect.'

George was certainly an architect on that day, an architect in the sense that in the midst of all the doom and gloom that was Northern Ireland during 'the troubles', he represented a light which shone brightly in the dark, a present day gladiator who unwittingly transcended sectarian divisions and in the process became an unlikely national hero.

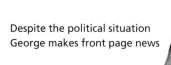

Despite the political situation George makes front page news

He's coming home! The world's greatest footballer is coming home to rest.
A football genius, a hero to so many, a Belfast Boy.

I never saw George play live but the clips just took my breath away. He could do anything with the ball and made it look so easy. He turned them left, then right, then left again. He was coming at them then passed them and the Belfast Boy scores again!

He brought his fellow Irishmen together in the name of football from the Falls to the Shankill – they all call him their Georgie Best.

I will leave the last words to you and words that you spoke – 'I loved entertaining the fans. That gave me the biggest thrill of all', George Best, 2005.

Brian Ambrose OBE   Belfast City Airport

As a boy the names of Best, Law and Charlton represented a golden era in football and like many kids my bedroom wall was covered with their photographs and the great Manchester United 1968 European Cup winning team – which I can still name effortlessly. George's sister Carol was a close family friend and when George moved to the US he gave Carol a couple of his famous green Northern Ireland jerseys. I was disappointed one Christmas morning to find this rather dated football jersey in my Santa Sack and initially worried that my pals would all receive the more up to date version. When my parents explained that this was one that George had worn at Windsor Park I was speechless.

'Will all passengers for...'

Hello . . . . and goodbye (see page 2)

Best Wishes   *George*

Printed by: BM Instant Print, 7 St. George's House, St. Georges Square, Huddersfield HD1 1LA.

Advertisement in the May 1972 issue
of George's Fan Club magazine

Many years later, shortly after George's death, I received a call from George's father Dickie. I was by then Chief Executive of Belfast City Airport and Dickie as ever was unassuming and courteous. Responding to unprecedented suggestions from the public to honour George, such as, naming the proposed National Stadium, erecting a statue at the City Hall or renaming the City Airport, Dickie said, 'The family would love to have the Airport named in George's honour but if you don't agree I understand and will never mention it to anyone'. A few weeks later over 70 of the world's media turned up to watch Dickie unfurl a banner to reveal George's famous signature on the logo of the new George Best Belfast City Airport.

While like others of my generation I marvelled at the unparalleled skills of a most gifted footballer, I also got to know a special family and in particular a special wee man – Dickie Best. When I was ask to speak at Dickie's funeral I counted it a great honour from a family I hold in deep affection.

George Best
**BELFAST
CITY AIRPORT**

The George Best

Dancers from Pro-Excel Move It project fly to
Manchester to perform a tribute dance to
George. It was perfomed on the 2nd anniversary
of George's funeral, 3 December 2007

JJ Gilmour   Creator and co writer of the musical *Dancing Shoes*

When I first started to write *Dancing Shoes* back in 2007 I knew I'd have to finish it one way or another. What a story! The more I read the more it became evident that five minutes of George Best's life seemed like five lifetimes to most of ours.

I began in his mid-childhood when he was dreaming of being a footballer just like a lot of young boy's dreams. George's dream came true like a Hogmanay firework display. I started with a song called 'One Day' and I knew I was onto something when a second, third and fourth song arrived shortly afterwards.

My dream also came true to write a musical about the life of one of the best footballer players in the world, but it was made so much easier with the help of one man's incredible life story, from the streets of Belfast to Hollywood and back. I know I'll look back on this in years to come as a very special day in my life, the day I decided to write about George's 'Dancing Shoes'.

One team – one religion

GEORGE YOU WERE A GREAT SON OF ULSTER AND AN INSPIRATION IN OUR TIMES OF TROUBLES THANKS FOR THE MEMORY R.I.P.

ONE MAY WONDER AT THE DELIGHT & PRIDE WHEN WE WATCH YOUR MAGIC FROM YOUR GOLDEN AGE. SIMPLY, WE ARE TRYING DESPERATELY TO KEEP YOU WITH US.

A true inspiration to all young people of Belfast and The World – Sport for All, Live forever George

The best shimmy-er there ever was. God Bless.

You were Northern Ireland's shining star, pride of Our Wee Country.

THE MOST NATURALLY GIFTED SPORTSPERSON THE WORLD HAS WITNESSED YOUR NORTHERN IRISH PASSION SHONE THROUGH IN EVERYTHING YOU DID – ON + OFF THE PITCH. LONG LIVE THE LEGEND!.

Words cannot express what this man did with a ball and he will be missed

you did us all proud. We'll miss you. Rest in peace

You were a Star that tumbled to earth. Rest in Peace.

GEORGE PATTERSON
BANGOR.

GLAD TO HAVE THE SAME NAME COME FROM THE SAME CITY AND SUPPORT THE SAME TEAM AS MY HERO GOD BLESS x

The BEST 7 player my dad ever saw.

PADDY
SPORTS DEV. OFFICER   BCC

AN INSPIRATION FOR A GENERATION + A TRUE GENTLEMAN AS WELL. YOU WILL ALWAYS BE IN OUR THOUGHTS.

The feet can't kick what the eyes don't, See.
float like a butterfly, Sting like a bee. LEGEND

GEORGE YOU DID THINGS BEYOND RATIONAL THINKING AND THATS
WHY YOU STOOD OUT AS A FOOTBALLER. YOU DIDN'T PLAY AT WORLD CUP.
LEVEL BUT WORLD CUP WINNERS PRAISED YOUR SKILL.
Heaven has a great Footballer.
God Bless.

YOU WHERE ONE OF THE FEW SONS OF ULSTER
WHO COULD & DID BRIDGE THE DIVIDE. WE ALL WANTED TO
BE GEORDY BEST. GOD BLESS YOUR FAMILY. —

My mum is a Blanchflower, and they were good
but you were the greatest!

One of the best in the world, you will be missed my all.
My thoughts are with your family. God Bless & Rest
in peace.
You were a hero, you were a legend, you were a genius
you weren't Brazilian you were Northern Irish and
you were ours, thank you George.

Well done George. You did a great job for all
of us. We will always remember you.

THE BEST REASON FOR BELIEVING IN AN AFTERLIFE
IS THE CHANCE OF A KICK AROUND WITH GEORGE.

True Legend, True Ulsterman
God Save George Best
May ULSTER NEVER FORGET

Davy M

George Best playing football was simply the most
thrilling thing I have ever seen in sport and I loved
him to bits. He had a heart and soul, he was brave
and brilliant and how the light shone when he left
the opposition for dead. The crowd often gawped in
awe at the flashes of brilliance before erupting into
roars of approval and appreciation. He was a kind
and brilliant, if flawed human being. Let him without
flaw cast the first stone.

George Best simply lit the fire in everyone who loved
sport, grace and beauty and approved of courage.

Thank you George and rest in well deserved peace.

Gifted   Best ever
Excellent   Extra-special
Outstanding   Superb
Remarkable   Talented.
Genius
Exceptionable

One Day at a Time!

Danny, Templepatrick

Belfast Child
Belfast Boy
Now the Belfast Legend
Off the pitch, a man with a weakness many of us share.
On the pitch a true legend.
Rest in peace George and thanks for the memories.

Words cannot describe your genius but I thank God that I
was alive to see you play. Your like will never be seen again

Beetles Made the Music
You Geordie Made the football Hu forever God Bless

R.I.P. georgie, BEST by name, BEST by nature,
Remembered by all the boys in the brandywell stadium, home of Derry City.

First Joey Dunlop, now georgie.
Both world class in their fields
In many dark days within our wee
country, you made us feel very proud
God bless.

Bus shelters on the Cregagh Road in December 2005
paid their own tribute

J. BEST 26.5.46 FROM ONE BEST TO ANOTHER GOD BLESS

Paul, Newtownabbey

He was the football genius, 'The Belfast Boy'
And to millions worldwide he gave so much joy.
He had humble beginnings, but never forgot his roots
And his skill knew no bounds when wearing his boots.
He was struck by an illness while still in his prime
But honoured many charities by donating his time.
George Best is a legend, whose name will live on
In our hearts forever now that he's gone.
Let's tell our children of the things he has done
And pass on his name from father to son.
He will always be remembered as a beacon of light
There'll be a new star shining in the sky each night.
Remember his football, not his so called demise.
I will remember him often with tears in my eyes.

A Brigade builder. Thanks.
R.I.P.

THE ORIGINAL BELFAST
GIANT
You helped put our Wee country on the map, we will do
you proud.

Thomas A Edison once said "genius is 1%
inspiration and 99% perspiration"
"Not in your case George"

Tom, Weymouth

On the day I left home in Belfast to join the Navy, I stopped on the way down to Plymouth at Old Trafford to watch Man U v Sheffield United. Bestie was sheer genius and the memory is clear as a bell – two of my better decisions – the other was George and Big Pat ripping the England World Cup winners apart.

The great Gordon Banks' face was a picture when he nicked the ball from him!

Pat Jennings, George and
Billy Bingham

British Broadcasting Corporation Manchester BH Oxford Road Manchester M60 1SJ

Telephone 0161 200 2000 Fax 0161 244 3122 Email nwt@bbc.co.uk

BBC

BBC North West

March 13th 2006

Dear Dick,

A blast from the past here. Gordon Burns from old UTV days although we spoke on the phone a couple of years ago. For the last 10 years I have presented the BBC's evening news programme from Manchester, North West Tonight. I have enclosed a copy of our programme both on DVD and VHS formats because I thought you and your family might like it as a reminder of George and how much he was loved in this part of the country. It is the live programme we transmitted on the sad day George died. This was the first and only time we threw out all other news stories and devoted the whole half hour to George and the reaction to his passing. It was, I feel, a very moving tribute to him. I had known George since the late 1960s when I first picked him up at your house in Burren Way when he was visiting you and took him on to UTV for an interview. There were many more meetings for interviews, either in Belfast or Manchester when I moved to Granada TV there, and also at various social gatherings. He was always warm, charming and friendly. And of course as a massive football fan I watched him play many times including that never to be forgotten international when he virtually played Scotland on his own! He was a true genius with the ball. It was therefore a hugely emotional time for me when I presented the programme I have enclosed. Towards the end of it, I read some emails that had coming pouring into the programme while we were on air, paying tribute to George.

PTO

Then I pay a short tribute myself and the emotion of the occasion started to get to me. My voice cracked right at the end and seconds after I said goodnight and a montage of George in action rounded off the programme ~~tears~~ were streaming down my face. It was just so sad to know he had gone. He is greatly missed.

For his funeral, Radio Ulster invited me over to join in their live coverage anchored by Wendy Austen and I found that hugely moving and difficult again to control my emotions. But I was particularly struck by your tremendous dignity and poise throughout what must have been a heart-rending service for you. I always found you to be a very friendly, warm and dignified man and I can't through that morning for all to see.

It was a privilege to have known George and a joy to watch him play. I hope our programme captured his genius and showed the love there was for him here in his second home, Manchester and the North West.

Please pass on my very best wishes to your family.

With very best wishes and happy memories

Gordon.

GORDON BURNS - PRESENTER BBC NORTH WEST TONIGHT

Tributes on the gates, Belfast City Hall

You brought inspiration + honour to the North. May God help all those who battle with your disease. Rest in Peace.

THE DEATH OF A FOOTBALLER.
THE BEGINING OF A LEGAND

Thank you for the Love and help you gave to others. Peace is yours God Bless.

A Wonderful life you did Belfast Proud — Rest in Peace
Great talent! We learn from your mistake

Once a star now an Angel

Never judge a man until you have walked a mile in his shoes

R.I.P. to one of the best sporting heroes of the last century.
He is comparable in every way to Ali and Pele.
His skill and precision on the field have not being matched since.

Carlsberg dont make footballers R.I.P.
But if they did they would make George Best!

Thank you for the memories.

Your talent was a gift. The gift you gave to us on this island was your generosity, your humanity, your presence amongst us which always served to bring us together as common humanity.

As in life, so in death, your departure has united us in the joy of your presence and of your departure.

May God bless you. You will always be remembered.

brought pleasure to the people of N. Ireland in its darkest days

BEST 1, BEAT 2, BEAT 3, BEAT 4 GOAL
THANK GEORGE YOU WHERE THE BEST.

To come from such a small population, to become one of the most famous people on the Planet – not bad for a Belfast Boy! Thanks for everything!

FAREWELL TO A LEGEND

NORMAN WHITESIDE

Manchester United and Northern Ireland

George was my inspiration. There was no one to touch him. He was simply a genius on the pitch. His name George Best, it couldn't be any better. The football that he produced for all the young kids to follow was absolutely amazing. All you wanted to do was grow up and be like George Best. He was a pure genius.

George with Manchester United striker Norman Whiteside and Glentoran Football Club mascot Stephen Chick. George turned out for the club on 14 August 1982

Tribute left at family home, Burren Way

George you'll be missed, but we'll remember with affection all the good times. You did more to unite people in this country than the politicians have done in thirty years, rest now.

The Elvis Presley of Football, icons of my youth.

The prodigal returned 'in style' trust you George

An inspiration to us all. To his family who have shown dignity at this difficult time our thoughts are with you.

I followed George's career, prayed for him throughout his last battle with his health and read countless words on his life and career, George had an amazing gift, but remained essentially modest and self-effacing throughout his life.

How many of us, so gifted, would have carried ourselves so unassumingly? It is for this that George won all our hearts, not just the ordinary people of Belfast, but from around the world. With this in mind, I offer the simple words.

'For the talent within the man and for the man within the talent.'

From an ordinary Belfast man

A Wonderful line you did Belfast
Proud — Rest in Peace
Great talent! We learn from your mistakes!

A talented, warm, witty man – you had the X-factor before anyone!

"WHAT THE CATERPILLAR CALLED THE END GOD CALLED THE BUTTERFLY"

This world was never meant for one as beautiful as you. —Vincent by Don McLean

Simply the "BEST"
The George Best Stadium would be a fitting tribute to this outstanding sportsman whose charity works has gone unmentioned.

YOU LIVED YOUR LIFE & ENJOYED IT – AFTER WHAT YOU GAVE, WHO ARE WE TO JUDGE WHETHER IT WAS RIGHT OR WRONG. THANKYOU FOR THE MEMORIES.

NEVER FORGOTTEN!
The face OF NORTHERN IRELAND
He gaves us something to be proud of.

Throughout George's career as a footballer he was recognised as someone who was above sectarian divisions, and because of that, coupled with his amazing performances on a football field, he will be remembered forever as, 'Our Belfast Boy – Our George.'

BEST IN HIS NATUR IN HIS FEET IN HIS HEART.

Wall mural Sandy Row, Belfast

Legend on feild and off!!
Hope they united the Ireland teams like you wanted!!!
Good nite sweet prince!!

THANKS GEORGE FOR YOUR GENIUS, & THANKS FOR BEING A BRILLIANT AMBASSADOR FOR YOUR COUNTRY AT A TIME WHEN, TO BE NORTHERN IRISH, WAS A DIRTY WORD R.I.P.

Who's Pele?

Your the Best!!

NI./1 Scotland 0   Thanks for the memories

went down fightin like true Belfast man

A genius footballer sadly missed
Pele was Right you were the BEST

We will remember the football George. R.I.P.

Much admired - Troubles are over.

ONE IN A MILLION
THE BRIGHTEST LIGHT IN THE FOOTBALL WORLD HAS SO SADLY BEEN EXTINGUISHED. I WAS SO VERY, VERY SORRY YOU HAD TO LEAVE US, BUT YOU WILL NEVER BE GONE, YOU HAVE LEFT A MILLION MEMORIES, ALL OF THEM GOOD.
"GEORGIE, GEORGIE, THEY CALLED HIM THE BELFAST BOY"
GOODBYE & GOD BLESS. XXX

Graeme McDowell, Portrush, Northern Ireland, US Golf Open Champion 2010

What can I say about George Best? I have always been a big football fan and as a kid George was my hero. Our family are crazy Manchester United fans, so much that my Dad named his first son after George! I wasn't that bad with a ball at my foot back in the day, but I soon knew that golf was the skill I was fortunately gifted with. I thought that if I was to become even half as good at my sport as George was at his, then I would go places.

I have always dreamt of following in his footsteps as a professional sportsman from Northern Ireland who became a global star. George's boots were very big ones to fill but I am honoured to have given it at least a shot to date. No matter how successful the remainder of my career might be, I can never come close to achieving what George did. He is sorely missed.

only one 24 CARAT

This mural replaced a paramilitary one in Portadown

Keep it lit big lad x

CIASS!

MAY YOU BE REMEMBERED FOR YOUR GREATEST DEEDS AND NOT YOUR WEAKEST NEEDS. ONE IN A MILLION.
1ST B'MENA NISC.

Great players better sense of humor, God bless

"Just a little bit special"

Both communities united in grief.

A flawed diamond, but what a diamond – at peace!

Such a naturally gifted footballer, the best, and to do it on those mucky pitches – phenomenal!

The whistle blew too early

It's not how far you fell, but how high you flew, and you soared!

GODS MADE THE GREATEST SIGNING EVER. FOR THE HEAVEN ELEVEN.
R.I.P. GEORGE

INSPIRATIONAL, WE'VE JUST LOST A LARGE PART OF OUR CULTURE.

It's nice to be important – but much more important to be nice – you raised me up, George. God bless.

GOLDEN BOOTS FOR GOLDEN BOY GEORGE

The gold-painted kid leather boots are not for playing in. They were presented to Manchester United's golden boy recently to mark the 250,000th sale of the George Best Soccer Shoe.
He was touring the maker's Leeds factory and a BBC-2 colour film unit was on hand to prepare a 50-minute documentary. George will keep the presentation boots . . . for luck.

Reproduced from Daily Mirror

**PRODUCTS OF STYLO MATCHMAKERS INTERNATIONAL LTD.
MATCHMAKER HOUSE, CLARENCE ROAD, LEEDS LS10 1TX**

MATCHMAKER BALL
In white vinyl with black honeycomb design made to F.A. specifications in weight and size. A superb quality ball with dimple surface for strenuous conditions produced for club training, education authorities and soccer players wanting a quality product for a reasonable outlay.

GEORGE BEST MATCHMAKER SOCCER KIT
BOY'S soccer kit in a choice of three attractive colours — includes a terrific set of FREE George Best transfers.

GB 60 Red jersey, white shorts, red socks
GB 61 Blue jersey, white shorts, blue socks
GB 62 White jersey, white shorts, white socks

PELE MATCHMAKER SOCCER SHOE
BP 120 BOYS' shoe handsomely styled in black leather with burgundy. Superb centre lace shoe cushioned through-out — padded collar and tongue. Sizes 2-5

NEW FIRST EVER ONE-PIECE TWO-COLOUR SOCCER SHOES

GEORGE BEST MATCHMAKERS
★ untearable eyelets
★ absorbent lining
★ ample support
★ foam padded insole
★ replaceable insole
★ completely new arch support
★ studs of proven shape — will not break off
★ flex-crack resistant
★ easy-to-clean just wipe with wet sponge
★ soft and supple no breaking in
★ exclusive toe area "a George Best" exclusive feature

GBC 74 BOYS' multi-stud   Sizes 13-5
GBC 80 MEN'S multi-stud   Sizes 6-11 inc. ½ sizes
GBC 75 BOYS' interchangeable stud Sizes 13-5
GBC 81 MEN'S interchangeable stud Sizes 6-11 inc. ½ sizes

Your touch was liquid Gold never has a player been so Gold.

The only man ever to nutmeg Johann Cruyff and a true gent. Enjoy it up there. Green + White Army.

Your sister said it the best – you aren't gone, you've just left the pitch xxx

The glory of life is not measured in moments of time but timeless moments. Rest in Peace.

Your name will forever be associated with magic genius & beauty. For everything, thank you.

Someone on heaven's dream team has just dropped to the bench! George Best Genius Love Robin & Chris

Although we mourn your passing
And we have to say 'Goodbye'
We're sure that you'll be playing
On that football pitch on high.

Best thing ta cum outa Northern Ireland since –.... uhh......um.... na wait he was da BEST!

Back on the green green grass of home.

Many had your demons but none had your feet! RIP.

I got butterflies in the stomach just watching you!

Your artistry on the football pitch will always be remembered.

Douglas Carson 05

From the sailing of the *Titanic*, *The Tales of Narnia* and the sounds of Van Morrison, east Belfast has made it's mark, but none more than the greatest footballer ever – George Best.

I never saw you live but everything I saw was magical – you never forgot where you came from.

You no longer need to fight for your feedom or peace – you have found it for eternity. Your legend will always live with us.

Rory McIlroy, Holywood, Northern Ireland, US Golf Open
Champion 2011

Every era has its sporting icons and for those growing up in the 60s, George Best would have been among the foremost. George had finished playing before I was born, but I have seen the footage and read the stories and realise just how great a footballer and popular a figure he was.

George thrilled millions with his unbelievable skills and I am very proud to have come from the same part of the world. It is also great to know he played for my favourite team, Manchester United.

You have to be very special to have an airport named after you – and George was obviously extra special.

Jonathan

I stood at RAF Aldergrove, just by the main gate, on my own. It was one of my last days in the RAF after nearly twenty years. I stood in my uniform with my Northern Ireland scarf. I didn't care what anyone thought.

As George passed by, having just arrived home, I raised my hand to salute, as is the custom, the tears were blinding me.

I remembered as a boy, George was at the Ballymena Show Grounds making an appearance in a friendly. My Dad got me through the crowds and I was lucky enough to meet George who signed my autograph book.

My memories are of a gentleman, who took time for the people who showed up to watch him. Even with those early memories, George left an impression and those very few seconds have stayed with me.

A man from whom we never saw the full potential, but they say what we saw on the pitch makes The Legend. For me, I remember a man who enjoyed 'his' people.

Stolen too soon. Rest in peace George.

GEORGE, SOMEONE SPECIAL BY HIS ROGUISH CHARM AND HIS AMAZING FANTASTIC DISPLAY OF FOOTBALL AND PLAYED JUST FOR THE FUN OF IT ALL GOD BLESS

MAY THE GREEN SOO OF NORTHERN IRELAND REST GENTLY ON YOU. GOD BLESS

Belfast weeps as the world mourns your passing May the Lord's face shine upon you George

THE WHOLE WORLD WANTED YOU GEORGE. BUT YOU BELONGED TO BELFAST. PROUD MEMORIES!

You lived with hell on earth, Rest in peace in heaven. There but for the Grace of God go I. Fellow alcholic!

Beside my mothers death bed was your autobiography "Blessed" - she only reached chapter 4. You were her hero - so I hope she meets you in heaven. God bless you both xx

David, Belfast

People come and people go, but George Best will remain imprinted on my soul. Ulster was given a great gift in the form of this remarkable wizard. Watching footage of him playing makes the hair on the back of my neck stand up and fills me with an overwhelming sense of pride, like no other football player has ever done before, or is likely to do again. A truly remarkable and special man, who did us all proud.

John, Newry

Homecoming from the swirling mists of memory comes, the Belfast Boy, embodiment of all our boyhood dreams. Flowing mane, twinkling eyes and magic in his toes. Zigzagging goal ward, into eternity: the mischievous smile, the precision shot, and the long sleeved fist in the air. From streetlights to floodlights, from the cracked pavement to the wide world. The creator of our memories, the magic seven in red, the beloved prodigal returning home to the arms he never really left. Applause! Applause! May the pipers play you to your reward.

George, Belfast

Today our whole country genuinely mourns its loss, but united, also celebrates your life. Not just the football genius, but the humble gracious person, who never forgot where he came from. Today is special, because the good has ultimately shone through and anything that tried to spoil the good has been discarded, as it should be. Thanks for the memories and for always being from Belfast.

George at Connswater Shopping Centre Belfast, 25 May 1984

BELFAST TELEGRAPH

George Best and me
Malcolm Wagner

In life, George Best always believed himself to be 'blessed' and we all agreed with him on that score. In contrast, I always considered myself to be 'lucky', lucky in the sense that I was able to share his early years with him, those amazing years before, during and after he'd managed to carve a world-wide reputation for himself as a sportsman, those years before the big problems arrived in his life to hurt him.

During those years we enjoyed wonderful closed-season holidays together to places such as the island of Majorca, Marbella on mainland Spain, and later, incredible trips to lots of exotic locations around the world.

My memories of George are of a funny, intelligent and mischievous lad, in fact, one of George's greatest qualities was that he always saw himself as being just one of the lads. In terms of being a mischievous lad, one of his greatest pleasures during his early years with Manchester United, seemed to be setting me up in order to get a laugh.

Waggy helps George to get the famous locks trimmed to send to the fans

I'll give you an example. As the attached photograph, taken from his 60's fan club magazine shows, I was his hairdresser. Prior to the photoshoot, where we dressed up in vintage clothing, George had decided, for a giggle, to use the article to inform his fans that if they wanted any clippings of his hair then they should contact me at The Village Barber Salon. Of course my name and business address was supplied. Needless to say, George never mentioned his intentions to me.

George had no idea of the response the article would have on his fan club readers but was not disappointed when we were subsequently mowed out with literally thousands of requests for bits of his hair. In fact, he thought the whole thing hilarious. Nevertheless, we were obliged to have a couple of apprentices collect and bind bits of George's locks together after every cut, place them in stamped, addressed envelope's and send them off to wherever. George's little joke occupied my entire salon for weeks. Whilst George laughed his head off at our predicament, constantly reminding me that it was just another example of what he called, 'Bestie power,' I seriously considered cutting all his hair off to meet the demand. In truth, I stopped short of actually doing anything for fear of removing what, after all, was his pride and joy.

The stories about George and his sense of humour are endless, as are those about a friendly, sociable and lovable man devoid of airs and graces but we have to remember that George was probably the world's first football superstar, a world class athlete and without doubt, a man who was truly blessed.

I was proud and privileged to be asked to speak at George's memorial service at Manchester Cathedral in 2006, my chance to pay my last respects for forty years of a friendship which gave my own life so much meaning and purpose. I only wish it could have lasted for another twenty years.

Northern Ireland versus Scotland international match. George and Celtic's David Hay

A tribute to
George Best

This book contains messages of condolence received on the UTV website from the many followers who appreciated the genius that was George Best.

Having two sons is great if god blesses them to play football like you we'd be very proud. Filled with pride for you family, you've came home to the best Belfast boy "Audaces fortung Juvat".

Never thought I'd be doing this!. So sadly missed, such a loss, what a great, great guy

George took football to the heights of art, and secured his place in the Pantheon forever.

Brendan, Banbridge

Well done UTV and U105 for the sensitive way you have highlighted George's life throughout this past week. You have helped us celebrate his life and George is filling the airwaves on U105.8 today. I'm sure there is a message in every song and George's memory is met with tears by the many.

Unfortunately my sister died almost two years after her liver transplant, just before George. The song I will associate with George is 'You're a Star' by the Lighthouse Family. This would be my personal tribute song for George. I just wish there is something I could do to help the family. They will need your thoughts and prayers over the next week and indeed the following months and years.

Please do not be afraid to cry, I did!

Ballymena Utd. FC.

George you guested for us in 1982. You captained the team against Motherwell. It was the proudest moment of my life. Thanks for the memories,

R.I.P George - you created the impossible - you made females interested in football. Rest in Peace George the Genius!

Football is changing now & not for the good of the game. Players like George Best remind us how it should be played with flair, commitment & a love for the game. It will be sorely missed

YOUR REPUTATION SPEAKS FOR ITSELF - HERE WE ARE 30 YEARS LATER TALKING ABOUT A FOOTBALL LEGEND WHO FINISHED PLAYING THE GAME AT THE AGE OF 26!

Nobby Stiles moves in to tackle George as he shoots for goal.
England versus Northern Ireland, Wembley, November 1965

Keith, Crossgar

Through the darkest days of Northern Ireland's conflict, George was someone who united everyone. We were all proud of George, even as he battled his illness. We will all remember his mercurial talent and his wonderful wit and wisdom. God bless you George. You may be gone, but you will live forever in the hearts of all your countrymen who revere you as the BEST footballer there has ever been.

Pete, Derry

Such was this man's personality and talent that he is remembered so fondly, by so many, years after he left the football pitch. An inspiration to countless footballers past and present and a man who lifted the hearts of people in Northern Ireland and gave them something good to think about during the dark days of the last 30 years.

David, Belfast

Today, players play on carpet and use lightweight balls, but you played on cow fields and used balls like concrete walls. Yet they still cry that they're hard done by. Whereas you were butchered, got up and started to fly. Now you are laid down to rest, forever more you will be the Best. A model player and a model gentleman.

Have a good rest Belfast boy. You will always be remembered.

Rab, Belfast

You stated seven weeks ago George that when feeling down you would often listen to Thin Lizzy's, 'The Boys Are Back in Town'. Well tonight we in Northern Ireland know our boy will soon be back in town. Thank you George for making my childhood more memorable with your silky skills.

God bless and keep you George.

Neil, Belfast

The first time I ever saw George was when I was a kid at a Northern Ireland pre-international training session in the grounds of Stormont. When the training ended George took off sprinting through the grounds with about 500 kids screaming and chasing him while he waved and had a real laugh. He did eventually stop and gave everyone with a pen and paper an autograph. It's a pity that the next time I see you at Stormont it will be such a sad occasion.

Rest in peace George. Genius. Legend already missed.

The Vernard twins, Jack and Ellie, with dad John, an ardent fan of George's

THE REST OF THE WORLD

Following that very famous game against Benfica in 1966, after which George was dubbed 'El Beatle' and then in 1968, again against Benfica, when Manchester United won the European Cup, George's fame rapidly spread throughout the world. His outstanding talent on a football pitch combined with his pop star good looks were an explosive combination, which added to his notoriety. Apart from his career with Manchester United and Northern Ireland, George played for other football clubs in places such as England, Scotland, Republic of Ireland, and Australia and most notably in the United States of America.

It is no surprise that many people from all around the globe paid tribute to George following his death, with some even making the journey to Belfast to say a final farewell. From Belfast to Brisbane, Manchester to Malaysia and further afield, this section contains tributes from many fans who all have one thing in common. They all held George, who came from such a small country as Northern Ireland, in such high esteem.

George Best: Tribute to a Legend
Translated into Japanese

International tributes

The Best artist   Parry Maguire

His feet drew the colours
All lined in a row
His boots used as brushes
His goals a rainbow

He mixed up his paints
on his canvas the pitch
And he weaved us his magic
With a swivel of his hips

A web spinning wonders
Deft strokes of the ball
Those sick came to watch him
For they went home cured

He rose as a phoenix
The bright shining star
Painted beautiful colours
On a grey football park

The kids loved to see him
At the theatre of dreams
He was like the pied piper
And his name they would sing

Now he's gone back to heaven
Tho' he left us too soon
But the world changed for better
When he laced up his boots

Steve and Fiona

We grew up in colonial Northern Rhodesia (now Zambia), both born in 1951, Steve a Livingstone boy, and I from Broken Hill. Little did we know, as children, that we shared a common memory – a following of Manchester United! I vividly remember my Dad, seated on a small stool, his ear glued to the radio, listening to a British football game. There was the shocking news of the Busby Babes' plane crash. Then came television in the1960s – and GEORGE BEST! The boys admired his football genius, and the girls swooned over him like the Beatles! Such was George's impact that, in November 2005, I stole some time out of our business, and sneaked home to watch his funeral on television. I was riveted from start to finish, tears streaming down my cheeks as the cemetery gates closed the world out so that his beloved family could privately lay to rest a son and brother and a father. They had shared most of George's life with the world, it was now their time! His send off was so poignant and historic, even the rain didn't let George down! The eulogies from The Prof, Denis Law, his sister Barbara, his son Calum, each touched a chord.

Then, not six weeks later, we met that very sister, in our shop in Ballito. Barbara and Norman were visiting South Africa, where Barbara had lived for some years in the 1970s. She had worked for our brother in a Hluhluwe hotel, and years later he had asked her to look us up. My heart missed a beat – could this really be George Best's sister? Wow, if only Dad was still alive!

Barbara brought George to life – she is the 'girl-next-door', and George was a brother, a boy from a loving family, I had lost my brother too. George was gifted with an incredible talent, yet blighted by a disease that is so often fuelled by the bitter/sweet of youthful fame, and that lost him the game of life.

Thank you Barbara for putting the final pieces to our treasured childhood puzzle. Thank you, too, for your time given to sharing his legacy so positively through his Foundation. Nelson Mandela knew how profoundly sport could unite people and transcend human barriers. I felt Ireland came out to do the same the day the crowds lined the streets of Belfast to bid farewell to their national hero who had come home to rest! May his legacy live on!

Desmond Tutu   Archbishop Emeritus   Cape Town

Many times I stand on the Cape beach and look across at Robben Island and remember the suffering endured there by our political leaders, including Nelson Mandela, during the apartheid era. On the edge of the island's high security compound is an abandoned football field. On Saturday afternoons, prisoners – including Madiba (Nelson Mandela) – were allowed to play soccer there. Many were young men who, as well as dreaming of a free South Africa, also had their sporting heroes in the old English First Division. There were prisoners who supported Manchester United, Chelsea, Tottenham Hotspur, Fulham, Blackburn Rovers and many other teams and avidly awaited news of weekend results and performances. Amongst the heroes who kept their spirits high was the young Belfast lad, George Best. Stories of his wizardry on the field – and his zest for life off it – filled the corridors of Robben Island prison.

Alas, his career was much too short and his star faded all too quickly. Yet, even now, we remember that star, shooting like a meteorite across the universe, and inviting us to make a wish. Like the Prodigal Son, George found his way home and we remember with gratitude, and great warmth – a sporting genius and lovable rogue – for brightening up our darkest hours.

Rest in Peace Georgie Best. My wish is that the Foundation set up to honour your life, will bring comfort and hope to many thousands who suffer the ravages of addiction in our world today.

Archbishop Tutu with Trevor Dwyer Lynch

Anonymous

I was a teenager living in Galway and my Dad was away working in England at the time. I desperately wanted to go to George's Testimonial in Windsor Park, but my Mum had three other children to look after and I was too young to go myself. I was however, determined to go and I cycled to the bus station in Galway about twenty miles from home. Although I bought a ticket, the driver wouldn't let me travel by myself, even though I pleaded with him and told him the reason why.

I was furious, but undeterred, I cycled to the outskirts of the city, found a piece of cardboard, bought a box of crayons and wrote 'BELFAST' on it. After about ten minutes a car stopped and I got in. The stranger asked me why I was going to Belfast and when I told him he started shaking his head. He told me about the 'troubles' in Belfast and worried that I may stray into an area where I shouldn't have gone. I was so frightened I asked him to drop me back to my bike and cycled all the way home again.

As it turned out, I watched the match at home and my brothers and mother who had no idea of my little escapade (and still don't) couldn't understand why I started crying when George scored that lovely chipped goal.

Little did they know that I could have been there for it!

HENRA
ANGERS
FRANCE

IL N'Y AURA JAMAIS UN AUTRE COMME LUI.

Colm, Churchtown, Dublin

I was a young boy in the 1960s; we got simple things for Christmas and birthdays. The greatest gift my parents gave me was a little Red shirt with a white collar. When I put it on I believed I was George Best, and went to sleep with my walls covered with pictures from the newspapers and magazines. Georgie, you painted my dreams with your feet! I am fortunate I saw you play in Dublin once. May God bless you and thank you for all you gave us. You will live in our hearts forever!

George in action at his testimonial match.
Windsor Park, 8 August 1988

郑苚,
SASA ZHENG   FROM ONE OF THE P.R CHINA

GEORGE BEST
MANCHESTER UNITED
           AND
NORTHERN IRELAND
         NOW PLAYING FOR
UNIVERSE UNITED
RUNNING RINGS AROUND THE STARS
AND SCORING GALACTIC GOALS.
NO ONE ON EARTH COULD STOP
YOU, AND NOTHING OUT IN THE
    COSMOS WILL
THANKS FOR THE ENJOYMENT
      YOU GAVE US, FROM
FOOTBALL FANS CLEETHORPES + GRIMSBY

I was born in Belfast thirty-four years ago and moved to Canada as a young lad. In all my time living in Canada, my Dad always told me about the great legend of GB. Now I've moved to Dublin and I'm visiting my Belfast roots for the weekend and I am honored to be here to pay my respects on behalf of me and GB's No1 fan, Paddy.

You were and are the Best!

Agim
      *KOSOVA
You tought us meaning of a word „Freedom"
Your work inspiration to many of us, we will miss you!
Rest in peace. We will meet again but not yet.

Wongayi Kauraro   I AM FROM ZIMBABWE AND WILL
                   ALWAYS MISS YOU GEORGE ONE LUV

We loved you back in Croatia too
Good Bless you!

Jag visste inte vem du var, men jag kom hit
och lärde mig att älska dig. Vila i frid Georger

We loved him in ESTONIA

George - you transcended everything - football ruled &
still rules. God bless Kyrenia Northern Cyprus.

JULIO MEDINA   PARA EL MEJOR JUGADOR DE
    SPAIN   FUTBOL DE LA HISTORI.

Sabrina Penna   L'Italia ti ricorda e Ti dona un saluto. Ciao!
Mauro   CIAO GEORGE, poeta maledetto del Soccer!

133

Per ardua ad astra – Through adversity to the stars.

From the Royal Air Force Football association – God speed

Stephen Way

Well … where would I start? Buying my first pair of George Best Stylo football boots, the glee when George scored six goals, the stunning European Cup triumph, kicking the ball out of Gordon Bank's hand? Could it be where Ron Harris failed (just) to cut George in half, or standing outside Stamford Bridge (the shed) and hearing over the speaker that George would not be playing, so sulking and ending up at Craven Cottage watching Fulham play Southampton reserves.

At the suggestion of my mother, whose holiday this was (an 80th birthday present no less) that we should go and find not only where George was buried, but also where he was born and where he first honed those skills what would make him such a worldwide household name. So it was, on a cold drizzly Saturday, that I found myself on the patch of green at the top of Burren Way, George's family home, with a ball at my feet. It could have been Wembley it could have been Windsor Park, as I set off across the sparse green grass, moving ball from left foot to right. The thrill took me back to my childhood. We all surely remember the magic as any patch of grass would suddenly become a major arena with which to show case our talent and here I was on that same grass where the greatest footballer in the world had first kicked a ball. Here I was nearing fifty, but still inspired by George and my childhood memories of the man, driving me on to ridicule myself in front of complete strangers.

My trip back in time didn't last quite as long as I had hoped, possibly minutes, as in that space of time, my rather boisterous young golden retriever, Bonham had been let loose from the car. It took me no time to realise that the game was over for me as Bonham had pinched the ball and I then had to take part in something resembling a Benny Hill comedy sketch. I chased Bonham, to all corners of the green, me panting and pleading to him to give me the (BLEEP) ball back.

Thus, my own tribute to George came to an abrupt end, but it was still as much a thrill as anything remembered from my own George Best childhood memories, to have finally visited and felt a little of the legend's own beginnings.

Bonham is still alive. Just!

Dave Kane

My Dad brought me to my first ever football match when I was just eight years of age. West Ham were playing Manchester United at Upton Park and I think the plan was for me to then follow the Hammers for the rest of my life, just like my Dad. I came away from that game wanting a Manchester United scarf because of what I had witnessed during the game. The genius of a player on the wing with his long black hair enthralled me all afternoon. This magician was giving the run-around to the local heroes of Moore, Bonds and McDowell, with skills which made me look on in total awe and wonderment. That day started my lifetime fascination with George Best. Consequently, all through my life I have supported Manchester United, watching them all over the country, at home and abroad.

The happiest day of my life was when I eventually met my hero. This was when I travelled to Iceland to watch United on a pre-season tour in 1982. George played for the opposition against United in one of the games. To actually have your photo taken with the great man was a total honour, but the best was still to come. On the return flight from Reykjavik to Glasgow, George actually sat next to me on the flight. We talked football all the way home and you can imagine how I felt. I floated home from Scotland to London.

The saddest day of my life was when George passed away. It was very ironic that as I stood there in Stormont on the day of the funeral, I now had my eight-year-old son standing next to me. I will always remember George, not only for what he did on a football pitch, but also as a real genuine, shy and honest man. They say you should never meet your heroes in case they never match up to your expectations, but in my case, they exceeded mine.

God bless you George. You are sadly missed.

TITANIC DAVE

Many expressions have been made over the years, but to me, the most wonderful was when Bob Bishop stated to Matt Busby in 1961, "I Think I've found you a genius." In life there have been exceptions in all different fields. George was certainly in this category. His intelligence was second to none. From his brain, to legs and feet, I feel his exceptional talent for football was emphasised by his intelligence.

I will always regret that I never had the pleasure of meeting George. When I went to Belfast to lay my wreath on his grave, it was a very emotional day. A couple of beers on the plane to calm me down and a taxi ride to Roselawn cemetery. Once finding the grave, that's when it all hit me and I had to go to the grave alone. As I laid my wreath at the headstone, that's when I simply broke my heart and wept like a child.

That's the influence the man had on me.

BELFAST TELEGRAPH

A mud spattered George is sent off in the game against Scotland. Windsor Park, April 1970

SEAMUS McCLELLAND

As with everything that I personally associate with George Best, sunshine and brightness play an important role. Of course George played on muddy pitches on cold November days up and down the country, but for those of us who watched him on Match of the Day or visualised him on radio back in the sixties, he will forever be our sunshine player. I first heard George's name mentioned one sunny day in 1963. My older brother Tom was arguing with his friends about who was the best footballer in England at the time. I was hanging around on the edge of the group when my cousin Paddy suddenly said 'from what I've read in the papers this morning, this young lad from Belfast George Best is going to be better than any of them'.

'George Best from Belfast'. To a young lad, living in the midlands of Ireland, that had a magical ring to it. Although I never had the pleasure of actually meeting him, that comment was the beginning of a beautiful friendship. Thanks to modern day technology, my son Danny who was born and lives in Germany, knows all about George and what he meant to football fans the world over. Excitement, thrills, genius and sunshine!

BELFAST TELEGRAPH

George is consoled by team mate Derek Dougan

John Warrington

I have so many memories of George. When we used to travel around the country doing his road show with Rodney Marsh, how he liked to host impromptu quizzes to pass the time in the car … we could never beat him! The last time I saw George was in August 2004 when we worked together on TV coverage of the Charity Shield.

My son was seven then and George sat him on his knee where he remained while we were watching the game being entertained by this wonderful man. I also have a photo of George with Robert from that day. He later gave Robert £20 and told him to buy me a drink to say thanks. I don't know if that was George's way of saying goodbye, but to this day, I still find that memory particularly poignant.

But my favourite memory goes back to 1994. My wife and I were having dinner with him when he produced a letter. It was from a man whose name I cannot remember. But he was a Romanian dissident who had been imprisoned in Romania during the 1960s under the Ceausescu regime. This letter said that to this man, who was denied his liberty, the thought of George and John Lennon kept him alive and his mind healthy during his worst times in a hell-hole of a prison. That George and John Lennon represented to this man the very meaning of the word freedom and that the two of them inspired this man and others caught up living in this dictatorship to work for freedom in their country.

While I was reading the letter, I saw that George had tears in his eyes. The fact that his own life had acted as an inspiration to somebody who was forced to live in appalling conditions, touched him greatly.

I wanted to come and visit George in hospital during his final days. But as a traditionalist I felt that those last hours should be for family and his longest and closest friends. But after he passed away, my son Robert and I went to the hospital and 'gave' George our lucky United scarf and placed it with all the other wonderful tributes and flowers. I truly hope that the luck that scarf gave to Robert and I has passed to George up in heaven.

Mick Wilcock

Quite simply, his name said it all. BEST, not just as a footballer, but as a person. He brightened up the dullest of games with his presence on the pitch. He had the supporters mesmerised with the skill he possessed through all the hard work he did in training. He made it all look easy, which for George it was. I'm sure he wasn't any happier when he pulled on that red shirt and Sir Matt said "Go out and enjoy yourself". He will never be forgotten by me and thousands of others. Simply the best!

Eugene Horan, Galway

I inherited my love for Manchester United through my mum's nine football crazy brothers, but it was their high praise and adoration of one man in particular that always fascinated me. That man was George Best. I listened in awe to their stories about the player who had it all!

My uncle Cathal brought me to my first ever United match, along with his son, my cousin Barry. I remember staying up late the night before the big game and Cathal telling us all about the genius of George Best. 'He made it look easy', he recalled. 'He could tackle, he could head a ball and not only was he a great goal scorer but he was a scorer of great goals!' My uncles, Kevin, Patsy and Keith met George in 1993. George was accompanied by an attractive lady and when Kevin openly asked, 'Will you marry this one Georgie?' George replied with a smile, 'If we win the league!' United did win the league that season for the first time in twenty-six years, but George didn't keep his spontaneous promise. Several photos were taken and the lads were none too pleased when they realised Patsy had forgotten to put a roll of film into the camera.

Uncle Keith once told me of his visit to his cousin in Birmingham in 1977 and how he admired a very unique figurine belonging to his cousin. The figurine featured Georgie in a typical dribbling pose with Billy Bremner attempting to win the ball off him … Bremner never did win the ball as Keith left for home with the 'Georgie' half of that figurine under his coat! So perhaps if that cousin is reading this he will finally realise just where George disappeared to!

My dear mum Maria was in her element the day we met George. My lifelong friend Dermot Hession was there with us. Mum always loved George and their photograph together still hangs in pride of place in her kitchen. My dad Owen always joked, 'He's the only other man you're allowed to have a thing for!'

In the summer of 2010, George's sister Barbara approached me about piecing together a video tribute to commemorate her brother's illustrious career. As a lifelong fan, this was an incredible honour for me and so I jumped at the opportunity to pay homage to my hero. The video was played on a giant screen in front of a sold-out Grand Opera House in George's native Belfast, at a special Gala evening to celebrate the hit musical *Dancing Shoes – The George Best Story*.

This was a very personal moment for me. I had come to George's home town and simply said 'thank you' in my own unique way. My tribute was received by rapturous applause from the star-studded audience. I was filled with both pride and emotion as George's family and former team mates all congratulated me on a job well done.

I can safely say meeting George Best is a moment I could never justify with words, yet I will spend a lifetime trying. For the incredible life he had lived and for that brief moment when he shared a fraction of it with 'me'! In years to come I will tell my grandchildren about the day I stood in the presence of greatness.

Immortal on the football field … Human off it …Your imperfections made us adore you even more, George. Your talent and character will never be equalled.

Oifig an Taoisigh
Office of the Taoiseach

December, 2005

Mr. Dickie Best
16 Burton Way
The Cregagh
Belfast
BT6 0DW

Dear Dickie,

I want to take this opportunity to extend my deepest sympathies to you, Callum and the extended Best family on George's untimely passing.

I was greatly saddened by George's death. As a lifelong Manchester United supporter, George was one of my great sporting heroes. My generation of football supporters were privileged to have seen George in his prime and I have no doubt that he will forever be remembered as not only one of the finest footballers this island has ever produced but as one of the best players the world has ever seen.

In my view, George was quite simply a football genius. I will always remember, as a teenager, sitting in front of the television enthralled by George's performance in the 1968 European Cup final which propelled United to such a famous victory.

George gave great pleasure to millions of football supporters across the globe. He was a man of unmatched football skills and great personal charisma and he will be sorely missed by so many people.

Oifig an Taoisigh, Tithe an Rialtais, Baile Átha Cliath 2.
Office of the Taoiseach, Government Buildings, Dublin 2.

On behalf of the Government my deepest sympathies.

Bertie Ahern
Taoiseach

On behalf of the FAI

John Delaney
CEO.

David J Blood
President

Tony Blair

Anyone who has ever seen him play will never forget it. He was probably the most naturally gifted footballer of his generation and one of the greatest which the United Kingdom has ever produced.

Oifig an Taoisigh
Office of the Taoiseach

- 2 -

I sincerely hope that the huge outpouring of warm tributes from around the world since George's passing go a small way in comforting you during this very sad time.

Both on my own behalf and on behalf of all my Government colleagues, I offer sincere condolences to your family.

Unfortunately, I cannot be with you on Saturday. However, like many millions of people throughout the world, I will be thinking of George. You and your family are in my thoughts and my prayers.

With my very best wishes.

Yours sincerely

Bertie

Bertie Ahern T.D.
Taoiseach

BUCKINGHAM PALACE

As President of the English Football Association, I Wish to Pass on My Deepest Sympathies and To Recognise George Best for what He Was – An Inspirational Footballer From Northern Ireland Whose Skills Captured The Imagination of Fans Around The World
H.R.H. The Duke of York

Oifig an Taoisigh, Tithe an Rialtais, Baile Átha Cliath 2.
Office of the Taoiseach, Government Buildings, Dublin 2.

UACHTARÁN NA hÉIREANN
PRESIDENT OF IRELAND

Mr. Richard Best
Cregagh Estate
East Belfast
Northern Ireland

29th November 2005

Dear Dickie

I was very saddened to learn of the death of your son, George.

May I offer you and all your family my sincere condolences at this very sad time.
I can only hope that your happy memories of George and the love and support of
family and friends will be a comfort to you.

George was indeed an extraordinarily talented footballer, and you can be rightly
proud of his many achievements. The legend that is George Best will long be
remembered.

May he rest in peace.

Yours sincerely

Mary McAleese
President of Ireland

ZCZC ESBX265 ESBT2100 8770112076
GBXX CO ESBX 033
BARCELONATF 033/30 25/11/2005 17:04:00

PRESIDENTE MANCHESTER UNITED S.C
M.U.F.C.
SIR MATT BUSBY WAY
OLD TRAFFORD,
MANCHESTER
M16 0RA

WOULD LIKE TO EXPRESS OURES TIPEST CONDOLENCES FOR THE LOSS
OF GEORGE BEST

FIRMA FLORENTINO PEREZ REAL MADRID C.F

ZCZC IUN900 DBB080 152/IH
GBXX CO IGMI 026
20100 MILANOFONO 26/25 25 2115 SENDER'S RISK

SIR MATTY
MANCHESTER UNITED FOOTBALL CLUB PLC
OLD TRAFFORD
SIR MATT BUSBY WAY
MANCHESTER
M16 0RA

SENTITE CONDOGLIANZE ALLA FAMIGLIA E ALLA SOCIETA' PER LA
PERDITA DEL GRANDE GEORGE.
ROSSI AUGUSTO

Teach Uí Aogáin,
Rae Mhuineacháin,
An tIúr,
BT35 8DJ

Chief Executive's Department,
O'Hagan House, Monaghan Row,
Newry, BT35 8DJ
Tel: (028) 3031 3034
Fax: (028) 3031 3045
Minicom: (028) 3025 7859
www.newryandmourne.gov.uk
E-mail:shiela.kieran@newryandmourne.gov.uk

Comhairle an Iúir & Mhúrn
Newry & Mourne District Council
Cléireach & Príomhfheidhmeannach – Clerk & Chief Executive
Thomas McCall

Ár dTag / Our Ref:
Bhur dTag / Your Ref:
Dáta / Date: M/21

1 December 2005

Mr Dickie Best
C/o Castlereagh Borough Council
Bradford Court
Upper Galwally
Belfast
BT8 6RB

Dear Mr Best

The Members of Newry and Mourne District Council have asked me to extend their sincere
condolences to you and your family on the death of your dear son George.

George was indeed an exceptionally talented sportsman who delighted the huge crowds who
watched him play football during his career.

The death of George has caused great sadness to many people, not only in these parts, but in
countries across the world.

George was an inspiration to many and will most certainly be remembered for the truly wonderful
football he played.

May I also extend my own personal condolences to you and your entire family circle on your sad
loss.

Yours sincerely

Mr T McCall
Clerk and Chief Executive

LV/KS

A few of the many official condolence
letters received from dignitaries,
Football Clubs and Associations from all
over the world

DEAR GEORGE,
YOU WILL ALWAYS BE
THE BEST.
LOVE FROM ALL YOUR
FANS IN TASMANIA,
AUSTRALIA. LONG LIVE
MAN UTD.

UNIQUE!

R.I.P. SHALOM ✡

Jone Solberg, Norway HERO!

LOVE FROM ICELAND

THE MASTER

Brentwood Bay
British Columbia
Canada.

As a teenager I was your greatest
Fan. And will always remember you as
the best Jennifer

Simm & Joe (from Malaysia)

He's the hero!!

I came over from Glasgow to pay my respects to GEORGE
and to convey my deepest sympathies to his family.

HUGH McILVANNEY Sports journalist

With feet as sensitive as pick-pockets' hands, his control of the ball under the most violent pressure was hypnotic. The bewildering repertoire of feints and swerves, sudden stops and demoralising spurts, exploited a freakish elasticity of limb and torso, tremendous physical strength for so slight a figure and balance that would have made Isaac Newton decide that he might as well have eaten the apple.

FROM A SCOUSER WHO WAS IN BELFAST WHEN YOU LEFT US
R.I.P

BEST ▽▽▽

BYES NAJLEPSZY ▽▽▽ POLAND

The 8th wonder of the world - George Best

LITHUANIA
PEOPLE
ARE
VERY
SAD

Thanks for everything, George. We'll always see you as the Belfast teenager that no one could stop. We'll also remember your kindness to others. God bless,
Tom
, Deansgrange, Blackrock, Co. Dublin

ON BEHALF OF NEW ZEALAND
KIA ORA MEA AROHA KIA KAHA !

MÓNICA·BAU-
BUENOS·AIRES - ARGENTINA.-
DESCANSA EN PAZ=

黄进华 C Shanghai·china 纪念 乔说·贝斯特. 伟大的球员铭记于人们心中

CHAUVEAU Pascal
Je suis trop jeune pour l'avoir connu mais à priori il était exceptionnel, alors GOOD LUCK AT HEAVEN!

Ich habe Dich erst über Zeitungsberichte der letzten Tage kennengelernt Ich wünsche Dir alles gute. A football-fan from Germany.

For all your faults George Best, you were a genius of your time. As a man of your age, I salute the greatness you brought to our era. And I weep with your family, Charlton and Law at your passing. If there has ever been a better forward line, I have not seen it.

Mike, West Lindfield, Australia

BEANNACHTAÍ MO CHARA GEORGE
SLÁN GO FÓILL — A TRUE CHAMPION

den BESTEN Fußballer mit dem Besten empfehlungen zum Familie

Paul, Midlands

George Best was an artist who didn't just play, but danced with the football that was glued to his feet for as long as he wanted it there. Blessed with unbelievable balance, like one of those Weebles that never fell down, he would torment defenders and then go back and torment them again just for the hell of it. The entertainment value when Best played was immeasurable; it was quite simply a privilege to watch. He made our lives infinitely better; he made us shout, sing, laugh and smile. But now we are crying for he is no more. Bless you George you were magnificent, the 'Best' footballer I have ever seen, or likely ever to see.

Rodney, Berkshire

I am from South Africa and when I was very young I remember my father and grandfather talking about George Best. It is only since I moved to the UK do I now understand what their excitement and joy was all about. They too have passed on but thank you George for helping me to see why they held you in such high esteem. Your legacy will remain for all to see.

Phil Brennan, Stockport

I was nine years old when I first became aware of George Best, it was 1968 and I was living at my Aunt Constance's house in Chorlton-cum-Hardy. I soon became aware of all things football in Manchester as Constance, had several lodgers in her big house, many of whom were fledgling newspaper reporters and on a Sunday over breakfast I used to sit and listen to their regaling of the games they been to the previous day.

I saw for myself at firsthand how good the two teams were as I was taken to Old Trafford and Maine Road on alternate Saturdays as the season neared its climax, although it was many years later that it became apparent that I had witnessed Best, Charlton, Law, Bell, Summerbee and Lee in their 'pomp'. My first introduction to 'real' football had been the previous May as my hometown team, Stockport County, received the Fourth Division Trophy on the last day of the season and, as I was to find out over the next forty plus years, in 'typical' County fashion they lost to the bottom club Lincoln City on their biggest day in years.

There were several things that I really loved about staying at Constance's, my regular visits to 'big games', my football education at the hands of the likes of James Lawton who was early into his career at the *Daily Express*, but most of all Constance had a television. On that night in May 1968, I sat in a full lounge at Constance's as we all huddled around the black and white television set to watch United against Benfica in the European Cup Final. George Best's brilliant goal as United won the trophy in extra time was the stand out moment for me.

Over the next few years George was always in the headlines, although unfortunately it was not always for football reasons and so imagine my surprise when one day not long after my seventeenth birthday I picked up a newspaper and there for all the world to see was the headline 'BEST signs for Stockport in the Fourth Division'.

I must have read and re-read the article a dozen times before it really sank in, George Best was actually going to play for County, MY COUNTY, at Edgeley Park. He had agreed to play in three games for County all of which were to be at Edgeley Park and that first game against Swansea couldn't come quickly enough for me. The first thing that struck me on the way to the game was that I had never seen so many people walking towards the grounds and when we got onto Hardcastle Road there was a sea of people the likes I had not seen before at Edgeley Park.

The crowd was over three times the normal we were used to at County and most of them were there to see George and he didn't disappoint anyone who had come to see him. Almost twenty minutes into the game, and having caused the visiting defence problems with two previous corner kicks, George sent over another in-swinging corner which Steve Potter in the 'Swans' goal could only palm into his net to give the Hatters the lead.

Ten minutes into the second half and George took on and beat three men, and to my young mind at the time at least double that amount, before sliding the ball into the path of Lee Bradley who slotted the ball passed Potter to double our lead. With less than twenty minutes to play the Edgeley Park crowd got the one thing that the majority had come to see ... a George Best goal!

George began the move with a pass to Ian Seddon whose cross was headed on and George, with his back to goal, volleyed the ball into the net for a tremendous finish to the loudest cheer I had ever heard at Edgeley Park. Swansea did pull two late goals back to give us all a few nervous minutes before the referee blew for full-time with County holding on to the two valuable points.

George's next game for County was a couple of weeks later, but my time in between was spent telling anyone who would listen that THE George Best had played and scored for MY Stockport County, it was an unbelievable feeling to know that all those years after I had witnessed the 'Belfast Boy' playing for Manchester United, he had played for County ... and he still had it!

George's second appearance for the Hatters came against Watford, and again the crowd was much larger than before his first game. George scored the opening goal and had a hand in a

goal for his fellow Irishman Ian Lawther as County picked up a point against the 'Hornets' in a 2–2 draw.

The last time I ever saw George Best play in the flesh came on Boxing Day in 1975 against Southport, he wore the number 11 shirt that he had worn against Watford and, although he didn't score in his final game, his presence again attracted a bumper crowd with well over 6,000 in Edgeley Park to see the mercurial Irishman play his part in a one goal victory thanks to a goal from Micky Hollis.

Whenever I hear people talk about George Best I know that I have been blessed to have witnessed one of the world's greatest ever footballing talents, both at the height of his powers with Manchester United and also for Stockport County where he played a big part in County picking up seven out of eight points and certainly helped the club to make some much needed revenue as over 20,000 supporters came through the Edgeley Park turnstiles to witness his three appearances in the blue and white of County.

God Bless you George.

Tropical Murphy's, Koh Samui

Paul Watson

I was at my home in Koh Samui in November 2005, celebrating a good friend's birthday and George's health was not getting any better. I was a life-long fan of George Best and considered him to be a wonderful footballer and an ambassador for Northern Ireland. When George passed away, every newspaper was printing his picture and telling great stories. I decided to collect them and make a wall of his life as a memorial to him upstairs in my bar Tropical Murphy's on the island of Koh Samui. It is there to stay and will only get more popular over the years.

'Tugboat' Billy, North Atlantic

Very sad to hear of the passing of this truly great man. A minute's silence has been observed by all on board here.

Stephen Patrick Evans

Dear Barbara

This is probably one of millions of messages travelling towards your monitor, but I wanted to let you know a few things. My father was born and brought up in Larne not too far away from Belfast. In his childhood he developed a passion for the game. No shoes, no money, but a ball at his feet. He always loved the game and had fun (since that's all that counts). He joined junior soldiers in his teens and on discovering the world with the British army he settled in Germany after many years. It was there that he got to meet my mother.

As my feet touched a ball for the first time, it was the name George Best that came to my ears. 'The most precious gift that football has ever seen ... one of the best if not the best.' Those were my father's words. Up to the present day we share the passion that George has brought to us. It was the same passion that brought me into training kids of 9–14 years of age. I just wanted to let you know the impact your brother had on many people crossing many international borders.

I was born in 1986. My father told me everything he knew about George Best ... just as I will tell mine someday. Next time you bring him some flowers or anything else just let him know that Stephen Patrick Evans and my father Michael Evens thank him! All my love and blessings to you and your loved ones. Take care.

Unique award-winning Scania T Truck designed by Chris Arthur from Sandy Arthur Training Services, Northern Ireland. Corgi has replicated this truck

John, Aberdeen

Best by a mile, the Belfast Boy with the magic feet skipped past defenders, a visual treat.

A dip of the shoulder, deft little flick. Making fools of opponents, with each little trick.

Would he go left? Would he go right? Before they knew it, he's out of sight.

Angry, they'd chase him, go two-footed in, but he would glide past them, flash them a grin.

On cold winter days, he'd make the fans smile, so all salute Georgie, the Best by a mile.

Gerald, California

I was eighteen when I saw George waltz his way past Benfica's goalkeeper in the European Cup. It remains an extraordinary vision in my mind today of his trademark economy of movement in the execution of goal scoring. He pioneered a unique art form at once so entertaining and surgical and seemingly so effortless, he single-handedly cut defences to shreds.

Gate at San Jose Earthquakes Football Club dedicated to George, spring 2011

Karl, Oxfordshire

In 1998 while I was sitting in a pub, this bloke with a soft Irish accent, dark hair and a bushy beard came and sat next to me. We chatted and then played some pool. He talked passionately about the game of football, he seemed knowledgeable and witty. He told me about the old game. We talked and played for a couple of hours then he left. When he had gone I thought what a nice bloke. Yesterday we all said goodbye to him. Thanks George, we will all miss you.

Jodie, Netherlands/Zambia

As a young girl growing up in Zambia, I heard about Georgie from my dad. Now thirty-five years later and living in Holland, I heard him on talkSPORT with Rodney Marsh. It brought tears to my eyes because I felt he was like right in our living room. This was my dad's football hero back in Zambia. He touched almost everyone's lives and may God bless him. Thank you George Best for being you.

George playing for Hibernians

TOOK MY DAUGHTERS TO SEE YOU PLAY – AND BRING MY GRANDSONS TO SAY GOODBYE – BETTER THAN PELE! THANKS GEORGE FOR THE FOOTBALL DREAM! Elsie + family + all of Scotland X

The girls and George

Belfast Boy   Joan McCabe

Belfast Boy, with those azure eyes
And the print of God's thumb in your chin
Beneath that dazzling smile,
You captured our hearts
You were poetry in motion
On those dancing weaving feet.
World icon, blessed with genius
With Mercury's wings on your heels.
Now a swaying ribbon of grief
Weeps along with heaven's tears
As sweet voices ease your passage home.
Even in death, you seduce us
As you are carried high
Crowned by fragrant lilies.
And then laid to rest
In the soft brown earth,
Belfast Boy, safe
In your mother's arms

A book about George Best without reference to the women in his life would be a bit like a book about football without mention of George Best.

Young, gifted, good looking and rich he was the first real superstar of football when he burst into the headlines in the Sixties injecting the game with a sudden and unexpected glamour. The Fifth Beatle, the papers called him. As one of the biggest celebrities of the day the media fêted him, men admired him and women adored him. And it would be fair to say that where the girls were concerned, the attraction was entirely mutual. George's 'private' life back then reads like a Who's Who of models, starlets, actresses and beauty queens. Especially beauty queens.

'I used to go missing a lot,' he once remarked, 'Miss Canada, Miss UK, Miss World ...' His girlfriends famously included a number of holders of the Miss World title. One estimate put the tally at seven.

the man who taught woman about football X

In his autobiography *The Good, The Bad and The Bubbly*, George dismissed this. 'It was only four ... I didn't turn up for the other three.' Danish model Eva Haraldsted sued him for breach of promise after he broke off their engagement. The actresses Susan George and Sinead Cusack and Miss USA Marjorie Wallace were among the famous early girlfriends. The singer Lynsey de Paul was romantically linked to him too. He was married twice – in 1978 to Angie (the couple divorced in 1986) and then, to Alex in 1995. (In 2004 that marriage also ended in divorce.) Both his former wives Angie and Alex attended his funeral in Belfast in November 2005 as did a number of his ex-girlfriends.

For all his faults George still retained a special place in the hearts of the women who loved him. After his death the actress Barbara Windsor told Piers Morgan in a television interview that she too had had a fling with the Belfast Boy.

'In the Sixties,' she said, 'he was so beautiful. He was fabulous.'
A sentiment which so many women would wholeheartedly agree with.

Lindy McDowell

George shows off his skills to Blinkers United Ladies Football Team.
Far right is George's fiancée of the time Eva Haraldsted, 1969

Carol MacPherson   Sister of George

'Our George.' What can I say about him that hasn't already been said? George was seventeen months old when I came into the world. We moved into 16 Burren Way in 1949 and our journey began.

We had such a good home and Mum and Dad were wonderful parents who loved and cared for us. There were no luxuries in those early years and George and I were by no means spoiled. Mum was a stickler for good behaviour and even more so when we went visiting. Even with that, George and I would still have our daily fights, which always ended up with us both getting punished by Mum.

When George began to play for Manchester United we were pleased with his success, but to us he was still just 'Our George'.

Many a time I think of those early years when we went on our family holiday to Groomsport and Bangor. Granny and Granda Withers with aunts Georgie, Joan and Uncle George. Uncle Tommy and Auntie Margaret with cousin Louis and Mum and Dad with George, Barbara and me. We stayed in wooden bungalows in a big field and can still see and hear the two Georges coming along the lane singing one of the latest pop songs with all their might.

Time marched on and George's visits home grew less and less as he became more famous, but we still loved him just the same. He was still 'Our George'

George decided that he wanted to come back to Northern Ireland to live and decided to buy a house in Portavogie where I have lived since 1974. I, of course was chuffed to bits. We spent some lovely times together during that period and talked a lot about old times. That was a very special time for me and I feel that it was meant to be for us both.

Many, many tributes have been paid to George down through the years since he died. A time that is etched in my mind always.

I thank my Lord for all his goodness to us both and look forward to a reunion one day.

Just good night 'Our George'.

Rosemary Mullen

I love football and was in George's fan club. My number was 1063. I did want to invite George to my wedding back in 1973, but my then to be husband (my rock) said he didn't want to be best man at his own wedding! I loved George, but not in that way. He will always have a place in my heart.

He was the Best.

Terry and Rosemary Mullen (née Harrison) were married at Abbot's Cross Presbyterian Church, Newtownabbey on 24 November 1973

We bring a lot of love with us George,
but the memories are ours to keep.
Thanks for creating them,
and being such a big part of my dads childhood
You're one in a life time and
he was privaledged to have experienced the
Skill that you put into the game
that is football.

Jenny, 16.

Membership No 1063

Name ROSEMARY HARRISON

Address 29, KNOCKENAGH
AVE, RATHFERN, DOAGHRD
NEWTOWNABBEY, N.I.

ABOUT YOUR CLUB

The George Best Club
Membership Card

glb

FIXTURES

Autographs

George Best

Collect the signatures of full international football players past and present on the space provided in your membership card. If you can obtain 30 different signatures you will qualify for a special competition—details to be announced later in the season.

DO NOT WRITE TO GEORGE ASKING HIM TO HELP

Rosemary's membership card to the George Best Club

FROM A <u>NEWCASTLE</u> FAN !!!!

Thank you, George

Thank you for all the excitement of your football, & all the laughs of your TV appearances, & for the inspiration of your life

With love,
Barbara xxx

Pam Shaw

I know only too well that I am one of the lucky ones who got to meet their idol and I also had the wonderful pleasure of watching him play. Both will remain in my heart as an experience that is be incredibly special. George was a huge part of my life, from growing up wanting to play like him to following his life with interest. He made growing up easy, because I did not get into trouble as some kids did and it kept me fit and interested in something other than school.

With the Foundation now set up in his name, his memory, name and legend will live on forever. The true fans who appreciated his brilliance and artistry will never forget him and I am very proud to say I am one of them.

Pam, Dartford

George you were the greatest footballer ever, fantastically handsome, but most of all a lovely bloke. When I was young I had to beg my Mum for £1.00 for the yearly subscription to the George Best Fan Club. You were such a big part of my teenage growing up years, and you gave me my love of football. Thanks for everything.

GEORGE
I LOVE YOU IN BIG WAYS
I LOVE YOU IN SMALL WAYS
I LOVE YOU THIS MINUTE
AND I'LL LOVE YOU ALWAYS
GOD BLESS YOU

FROM THE ONLY BRUNETTE
TO TURN YOUR HEAD

XXXX

to Georgie

Ireland lost a Son
Football lost a legend
and I lost my
sweetheart

Love Maggie xxx
xx

MANCHESTER UNITED MUSEUM

George Best. His coat.

George's Boutiques Manchester

EDWARDIA
KING STREET · MANCHESTER

GEORGE BEST ROGUE
MARKET WALK · MANCHESTER

Championship Match? George tries his hand against the strong left arm of Heavyweight Boxer Brian London. Brian had just popped in for a browse round Edwardia. He agreed that the selection was certainly a knockout. You never know which famous personalities you meet at George's city centre boutiques.

Linda Galleozzie

My life of admiring George began in 1966 when I was nine years old. It was at the time when he was photographed in a sombrero coming off the plane, headlines read 'El Beatle' and it was my late father who inspired my admiration of George from that moment onwards. My dad who was a very proud Irishman said that this great little Irish boy was something special and how right he was! Ever since then, my whole life has been dedicated to following his life and collecting his memorabilia. I had the greatest privilege to have met him on three occasions in his later years and on the last occasion in 2004, he remembered my name.

George was very much indeed a special and unique person who touched the hearts of many and never changed with all his fame and magical talent on the football field.

He is a Genius and his Legacy will live on through the great work of the George Best Foundation.

God Bless You Bestie! x

Lynsey (aged 14)

I never knew George as I was still quite young when he died, but nevertheless it was as if I knew him my whole life. There was something about him that said he was friends with everyone no matter what. On the day he died, he pulled everyone together and we all became one to grieve for the one and only George Best. On the Saturday of the funeral, I was standing outside Dickie's house with my family and although I wasn't born when the legend was at his best, I was there when the legend was put to rest. I'll never forget that day no matter what and whatever happens through my life, I can always say I was there. My Dad told me all the stories about George and I believe that it has made me aware of what an amazing man he was. A true gentleman and I am sure he is now in heaven playing football with the angels. I would like to thank George for showing us what real football is about.

GEORGE BEST COLOURING COMPETITION
PRIZES! PRIZES! PRIZES! PRIZES!

FREE George Best picture card/entry form with every packet

Star Prize

Best Potato Crisps
Cheese 'n Onion
3p

MANCHESTER UNITED MUSEUM

fore.
AFTER SHAVE
George BEST
GROOMING AID

MANCHESTER UNITED MUSEUM

George signs autographs for female fans in Royal Avenue, Belfast, prior to the game against Russia, September 1969

Geraldine Newell

I grew up in Holywood, Northern Ireland, and now live in the USA. I had the great pleasure of meeting George at Whispers Night Club in Groomsport back in the late 70s. I have always been a fan of Georgie and cried many nights around the time of his death. My American husband and daughter to this day, joke about how I cried about his death. They don't understand the feelings we Irish have when someone you really did not know, dies, but truly loved. They like to keep me going about how much I cried over someone I only met once. He was such a gentle person and a superstar from Belfast.

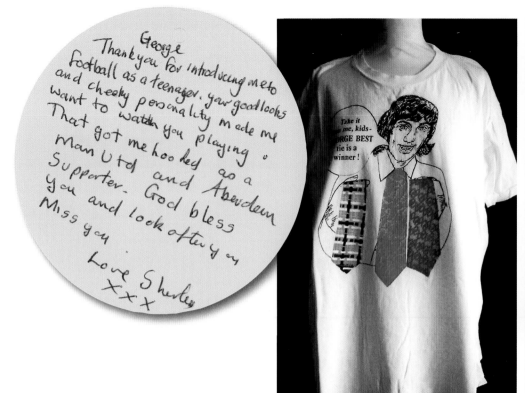

George
Thank you for introducing me to
football as a teenager, your good looks
and cheeky personality made me
want to watch you playing.
That got me hooked as a
Man Utd and Aberdeen
Supporter. God bless
you and look after you
Miss you.
Love Sheila
XXX

Dearest George
A true genius of the kind
we will never see again
You are and always will
be My shining Star
Forever in my heart
You were and always
will be
      Simply the Best
Fell asleep to soon
  Love always
  Cathy x

Diane, Costa del Sol

In my late teens in the 60s, I was practically forced to watch a football match on TV by my boyfriend at the time. I can tell you this was something I did most reluctantly and grudgingly. The game featured Manchester United and I can still remember becoming absolutely mesmerised and transfixed by the magic of George Best, I have been a football fan ever since! Thank you George. My heart goes out to his family who have so much to be proud of. Not only was he the best footballer the world has known, he was also a very intelligent, articulate man who had a terrific sense of humour.

Carole, Lincolnshire

I was one of three girls growing up in the 1960s. I watched football with my dad and fell in love with Manchester United and Georgie Best. For my twelfth birthday I asked for a Manchester United shirt, which I wore as a mini dress. You were my first love George and you shall be my last, the very Best, and a shining star who will never be forgotten. X

Laura
Newtownabbey Strikers
W.F.C.

GENIUS, LEGEND, PHENOMENON, HERO, MAGICAL, ADORED BLESSED, MODEST, INSPIRATIONAL, UNFORGETTABLE. THE BEST. R.I.P. GEORGE BEST X.

BICARD Caroline   Quelle Émotion dans ce pays

BELFAST TELEGRAPH

Beryl Hammond

I was crazy about George in the late 60s early 70s and had so many posters of him on my walls. Those eyes – he was so handsome. Because of George I have supported Manchester United all these years.

Lyndsey, Amersham

I wasn't old enough to see you play, and I didn't even follow football from a very early age, but my brother Neil did. I can remember him going to a fancy dress party dressed as you, and raving on about you. He always thought you must be something really special, and you were. From that point I was intrigued by this footballer George Best. What I would like to say is my brother and I have become distant in recent years to the point of hardly speaking, and for the first time in months we have been in touch and it was to ask each other how we were going to pay our respects to you. The legend. It is easy to see the glint in everyone's eye when your name is mentioned and there will never be another player who is half the man you were. You were so humble, a true icon.

Rest in peace, as you deserve to.

BELFAST TELEGRAPH

January 1968

We watched George when we were young. Mum loved him as well. We are now Chelsea and Arsenal fans. But George Best was the best footballer ever. We loved watching Man U when he played.

Kathleen and Margaret

Celia, Dublin

You have given so many wonderful memories to thousands of people. The 25th November 2005 will stay in my memory forever. The world lost the greatest football legend. I will never forget you George. You were my idol from a very young age.

Goodbye and God bless

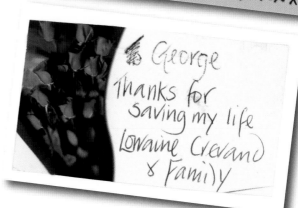

I watched you play your football here, in the 60's. How lucky was I? How lucky were we all? Rest in Peace George — You beautiful, blue-eyed, Irish Genious. God Bless. Carol C — Man Utd Supporter. + family. x x x x x x x

George Thanks for saving my life Lorraine Crevano & family

Dearest George
You were the greatest and most talented Player ever, you were the most beautiful man I have ever seen, You have always been my Idol, you always will be. I miss you so much already, God bless you, with all my love Karen Beat
Billericay
ESSEX
xxx
xxx

2006-06-26.
Monday.
Dear George,
This is just a short note to say finally I am able to let you go. This trip to Belfast has been a chance to search my soul & now I understand why I was so interested in your life. I tried to cling to you, but no longer can do that. Unfortunately I now know the damage alcohol can do to life. I don't need that any more in life.
There is no doubt that you

were a wonderful footballer & very handsome man, but my heart has to let you go. At last I am complete enough to do that. I hope that sometimes you will look over me & help me through these horrible times. God bless your spirit & soul George.
Thanks for the memories.

Much love -
Rosie xx
(CORK).

Belfast
City Hall
1906 – 2006

Irene, Chesterfield

God bless you George. Today, we have all shed a tear. In the late 60s you were a god to the boys and us girls fancied the pants off you. Through the years you were always a pleasure to watch, either on the field or in interviews. Calum, take solace in these messages as your dad was a good guy and was loved by the ordinary man in the street.

"SIMPLY THE BEST"

I have adored you from the age of 12 I am now 50 you are my hero, my heart is breaking an angel only lent, you have inspired so many.
So sadly MISSEd loved by so many
GOD BLESS
Lynda
xx

I've never been a football fan - but what I've seen over the past days I wished I had been.
Lorraine

Dear Mr Best,

I drove by the hospital most nights thinking of you and praying for you. My wish to meet you has not come true but you have left us with many wonderful thoughts.. I have always admired you.

May you rest in peace

Love Susy

x

form 1 girls
from B.R.A.?

A True Legend you put us on the map rest in peace forever

Danced with you on children in Need
You can now Dance wal tb Angles
You can never be replaced. Anya

George, the love of my life. 1967 NI v Scotland, I was there aged 12. You made me fall in love with football. You are the best I have ever seen. Hope you are happy and at peace, you deserve it. Love Ann xxxxx

Didn't know who you were until a week ago and now I wish I had …

A Canadian girl

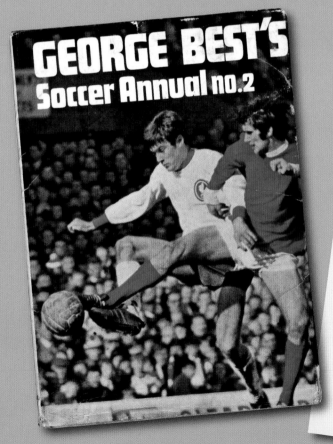

GEORGE BEST'S
Soccer Annual no.2

IN MEMORY OF GEORGE BEST

I AM A LADY IN MY 60s AND YES I WILL ALWAYS REMEMBER WATCHING GEORGE PLAY WITH THE UTMOST PRIDE AND STRANGLY ENOUGH AFFECTION, I WAS TOTALLY MESMERIZED TO SEE THE WAY HE COULD CONTROL A BALL ABSOLUTE GENIUS. EVERY TIME I HEAR HIS NAME I SEE HIM ON THE FIELD, WE ALL LOVED GEORGE AND WE WILL NEVER FORGET THE NAME MANCHESTER UNITED, THAT WAS WHERE HE LOVED TO BE, ONE OF THE PLACES WHERE HE WAS HAPPIEST.

I LIVE IN GLOUCESTER HAVE NEVER BEEN TO UNITED BUT I DO HOPE ONE DAY TO MAKE THAT VISIT AND HOPEFULLY JUST TOUCH THAT GRASS WHERE GEORGE ONCE PLAYED. MY EYES TODAY HAVE FILLED WITH TEARS ON AND OFF SAT NEAR THE RADIO LISTENING AND WAITING FOR THE DREADED WORDS " GEORGE HAS PASSED AWAY".

GOOD ON YOU GEORGE, LETS HOPE YOUR GOING TO A BETTER PLACE, SORTING YOURSELF OUT A BEAUTIFUL ANGLE NO DOUBT, GOD BLESS AND TAKE YOU TO THAT PLACE WE WILL ALL ONE DAY FOLLOW YOU TO. I HOPE WHEN I MAKE THAT JOURNEY GEORGE WILL WELCOME ME AND ALL HIS OTHER FANS THROUGH THOSE GOLDEN GATES WHERE HE MAY ONCE AGAIN BE KICKING THAT BALL.

GOD BLESS YOU GEORGE AND THANKS FOR WONDERFUL MEMORIES.

GLOUCESTER LADY.

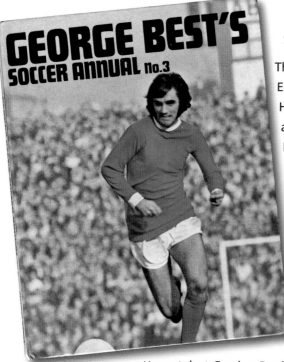

Sarah Pearson

The day before my fourteenth birthday, Northern Ireland was at home to England. My Mum warned me I was not allowed anywhere near the football. Her concern was understandable, the crowd carried you along with police and army, guns in hand, on every street corner. However, I got a lift to Windsor Park and made my way to the fence on the side of the pitch and when the teams emerged it was so easy to pick out George from the line of green jerseys. No one wore that jersey with such style. No-one was as handsome!

The linesman, running the line in front of me was biased towards England. He had dark ginger hair and sported an unruly beard. He made several bad calls against Northern Ireland. The supporters slated him, 'get some glasses Santa.' When George ran past me I was in seventh heaven and when he took a throw in I raced up and down that side of the pitch with George. There had been a goal attempt, but Gordon Banks had got to it and the Northern Ireland team members were walking back down the pitch, when George turned and marked Gordon Banks as he held the ball in his hands ready for a goal kick. We all watched in silence … what was he doing? Gordon turned this way and that way, every time marked by George and when he released the ball to kick it downfield, George got to kick it first, sending the ball over their heads. Both George and Gordon Banks raced to get the ball, but Banks was outpaced by George, heading the ball into the empty goal. The crowd went mad! Everyone stood and watched in disbelief, we cheered not only for the goal, but for the inventive goal that it was. Gordon Banks raised his hands, Bobby Moore walked to Gordon Banks, the referee, looked as bewildered as the rest and then looked towards the linesmen. They both shook their heads and the referee declared the goal disallowed. The full wrath of the crowd's anger was released onto the officials, especially the beardy guy on our side of the pitch!

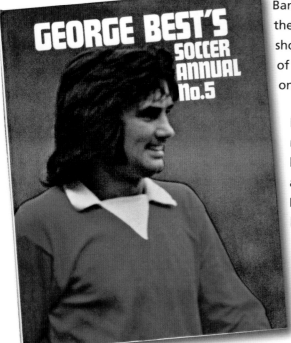

Noel, my brother-in-law to be, was football mad, he ran his own football team and he refereed, but being a professional, he didn't go to the stands like the rest of us, and I knew that I would be lost in the crowds and Mum would be none the wiser. However arriving home later that night, Match of the Day was on TV and Mum asked me where I had been that day. Over her shoulder I could see Noel, slightly shake his head … But bravely I lied, 'in town'. So that wasn't you hanging onto the fence at Windsor Park yelling like a hooligan? I was gutted. How did she know? I found out later the camera had panned the supporters and caught me full in its lens and as a result, I was grounded on my birthday … but it was so worth it!

The Funeral

3 December 2005

BARBARA McNARRY

(Words spoken at funeral)

Do not look on George as gone. He has only stepped off the pitch.

Most of us know just how exceptional George was because of his incredible skill at football. A gift that he loved. A gift which gave pleasure and thrills to millions over the years. He was an exceptional man. A man of grace both on the field and off. A sportsman of enormous stature and a friend to all, to whom he gave freely of his time and energy. Something which was sadly not always recognised by others.

During your last hours Professor Williams told the world you were coming to the end of your long road. It was a road that took you from Belfast at the age of fifteen, to what was to be your destiny. It took you to far off places and glittering heights. At times it was a hard road, but that road brought you back to the city, to the people and back to the family who loved you most of all.

Immaculately turned out players from Cregagh Rangers Football Club form a guard of honour on the steps of Stormont, 3 December 2005

DOCTOR AKEEL ALISA

(Words spoken at funeral service)

George Best showed the beautiful side of football and turned it into a living art. He wasn't very tall, he wasn't very large, but there was nothing he couldn't do on the pitch. John Lennon sang Imagine. George Best practised Imagine. The Beatles brought music to our ears. George Best brought magic to our eyes. What he has done for the game of football will never be forgotten.

On a cold chilly November day, George Best left us way too soon. My wish is that you find peace. God bless you and thank you for being who you were.

Funeral cortège on the Cregagh Road, Belfast

Dear Mr Best,

I write to record my personal thanks and those of my friend Bill for the very kind and considerate gesture made by your family in inviting individuals from the crowd to join you inside Stormont on the day of your son's funeral. It was with a great sense of disbelief and honour that we joined with those inside in giving thanks and paying tribute to one who made my teenage years especially memorable. The first time my father took me as a thirteen-year-old boy from Maghera to Windsor Park to see a World Cup qualifying game with Switzerland in 1964 will live long in my memory. I had the privilege to attend the famous game against Scotland in 1967 when George gave what many believe was the finest performance ever by a player in a Northern Ireland jersey. Truly marvellous.

I captained the team up in Tobermore for many years, but missed the opportunity to play with George when he guested for them in the Irish Cup. I spoke recently with the Tobermore manager of the time and he explained how apprehensive he was about giving a team talk before the game with George present. He shared with me that it was almost as if George sensed his anxiety and said 'Don't worry; today I am just one of the boys here'. Typical of George, so unassuming.

I have a copy of the Order of Service from the funeral together with the rain sodden invitation calling me to join your family for the service. It is a very special reminder of a day which will long be remembered for football fans everywhere.

I commend the excellent work which your daughter, Barbara and her husband Norman are undertaking in seeking to ensure that George's name is honoured through the work of the George Best Foundation. It is right and fitting that one who brought excitement and enjoyment to so many should be honoured in this way.

Yours sincerely,
Ronnie

Funeral cortège
leaves Stormont,
3 December 2005

Ireland's Saturday Night

THE FINAL JOURNEY

A sports edition of
The Belfast Telegraph

Special edition

SATURDAY, DECEMBER 3, 2005   109TH YEAR   PRICE 55p   www.irelandssaturdaynight.co.uk

JUST WATCHED BESTIES FUNERAL – WHAT A
FANTASTIC SHOW OF RESPECT FOR THE
'BELFAST LAD' XX

My wee son Ben was honoured to be part of
the guard of honour with C.B. football team
he says he'll never forget george "we won't let him

Councillor Jim Rodgers   Fondly Remembered. It was a pleasure to have known
                              you.
                              God Bless.

Came all the way from Doncaster just
for you George, to say our last goodbye.
Rest in Peace my shining star love alway X.

Colin   Witnessing the Love, emotion & affection the
From glasgow   Northern Ireland people have for you has been
                 amazing – they have done you proud today

Tributes at Burren Way

Dear Norman and Barbara

My ten-year-old son Justin and I write to you as two of the members of the public specially invited by your family to attend the funeral service of George and afterwards to go to La Mon Hotel, where we met with you.

I wish to express our great appreciation for this wonderfully kind gesture and to let you know that it was such an honour and privilege for us to have been there.

I obviously have enjoyed George's great footballing skills over the years; however, Justin has only just been captivated for the first time by the video clips being shown over the last weeks and months. Another generation has become aware of the great skills and this is what George would have wanted.

Justin asked me to take him to the funeral and said that he would like to meet Calum in particular. I explained that we wouldn't be able to meet any of the family, but that we would be part of a very large crowd gathered to pay tribute to George and celebrate the good which he brought to people.

We queued from early morning and entered Stormont grounds delighted and pleased just to be there, even on a cold and wet day. You cannot imagine our great joy and excitement about being approached and invited to move forward to join the service, which was such an appropriate and moving tribute to George. Justin even got to meet Calum and many others.

We thank you again for this memorable red letter day which will remain with us for years to come. Thank you for your kindness.

I would like to take this opportunity to wish all your family every blessing in the weeks and months that lie ahead.

Yours sincerely,
Philip

George Best Foundation – the work goes on

The Foundation aims to:

- Promote and encourage a healthier lifestyle among young people through football in particular, but sport in general;

- Support groups working with young people and/or adults who are already experiencing alcohol or drug problems either on a personal level or within their immediate family;

- Support vital medical research into illness particularly associated with alcohol misuse.

To achieve these aims the Foundation will:

- Promote a healthy lifestyle through football/sport based initiatives;

- Provide education and advice on drug and alcohol misuse through youth and community initiatives;

- Provide education and advice on diet and nutrition through youth and community initiatives;

- Advocate for the benefits of a healthy lifestyle at events and initiatives and through the media; and

- Provide funds to assist with medical research into illness particular associated with alcohol misuse through universities and other medical establishments.

The Foundation is committed to providing charitable funds to everyone regardless of age, ethnicity, gender, sexual orientation, nationality and political or religious opinion.

The Foundation will focus on providing charitable funds for the public in the United Kingdom and Ireland and will also support a small number of international projects.

Sports equipment to nine primary schools in Uganda

Victory at the transplant Games, Australia 2009

GARY HANCOCK

Achievements to date

The following is a brief outline of the financial support which has been given by the George Best Foundation since its inception in April 2006. The George Best Foundation strives to give each young person the unique opportunity to learn and develop skills through the power of sport in social inclusion programmes.

£100,000 to the Foundation for Liver Research, University College London. This enabled the employment of a research scientist for a period of two years.

£30,000 'Best Way Forward' event 2008 was a cross-community football-based initiative for 950 young people including those with disabilities. Working in conjunction with the Irish Football Association, every child was also given drug and alcohol awareness education by the Forum Against Substance Abuse.

£30,000 'Best Way Forward' event 2009 was a two week multi-sport-based initiative working in conjunction with Eddie Irvine Sports. 1,200 young people, including those with disabilities, were hosted and given educational advice on nutrition as well as drug and alcohol misuse by various health agencies.

£20,000 'BEST Way Forward' event 2010 was a one week multi-sport-based initiative working in conjunction with Eddie Irvine Sports. 800 young people, including those with disabilities were hosted and given educational advice on nutrition as well as drug and alcohol misuse by various health agencies.

£20,000 'BEST Way Forward' event 2011 was a one week multi-sport-based initiative working in conjunction with Eddie Irvine Sports. 800 young people, including those with disabilities were hosted and given educational advice on nutrition as well as drug and alcohol misuse by various health agencies.

£15,000 'Belfast Giant's H.E.R.O.S' (Hockey Education Reaching Out Society) was an initiative, which brought together 35 'at risk' young people in a cross community/cross border programme. The project provided each young person with experiences to encourage them to develop self trust, self-esteem, confidence, personal aspirations and respect for 'others'.

Pupil from Ugandan primary school

£15,000 George Best Memorial Trophy 2010. Working in conjunction with the Manchester United Foundation, this money was invested to bring together 36 teenagers aged 16–18 from Belfast and Manchester in a cross-community and multi-cultural football competition.

£15,000 George Best Memorial Trophy 2011. Working in conjunction with the Manchester United Foundation, this money was invested to bring together 36 teenagers from Belfast and Manchester in a cross-community and multi-cultural football competition.

£6,000 to Transplant Sport UK towards the cost of assisting four teenagers to attend the World Transplant Games in Australia, August 2009.

£4,000 to Soccer Sight project to supply an electronic audio transmitter/receiver system which brings quality commentary at sporting events to blind and partially sighted people, by specially trained commentators.

£2,500 to Abaana Ministries to supply sports equipment to nine primary schools in Uganda and level an area to establish a grass soccer pitch at the Dr Andrew McAvoy School.

£1,000 to Ballysillan Youth for Christ towards their 'Blue House' scheme which gives support to young people who have already been experimenting with drugs and alcohol, or who have been affected by other family members who do.

£1,000 to Hillsborough Junior Football Club for their annual cross-community football tournament.

£1,500 over a three year period to Mpondweni Primary School, South Africa for sports equipment.

£500 to St Anne's Primary School, Northern Ireland to assist with their drug/alcohol awareness poster campaign.

£500 to Carryduff Colts Football team to purchase a football strip to travel to Barcelona to participate in a tournament.

The George Best Foundation team who participated in the George Best Memorial Trophy with Manchester United player Gary Neville, 12 April 2011

www.georgebest.com

George loved to paint. This is thought to be the final one which he did before his death

Last ever live interview in September 2005

Well, I know what the fans will think. They'll forget all the rubbish when I'm gone and they'll remember the football. It's as simple as that. As long as they remember the football and if only one person thinks I was the BEST player in the world that will do for me. That's what it's about as far as I'm concerned.

God saw the road was rough, the hills were hard.
He closed your eyes and whispered
'Peace be thine'.

Neil Vacher

When George made his debut for A.F.C. Bournemouth in 1983 his appearance immediately doubled the club's previous home attendance. Unfortunately though, injuries meant his stay at Dean Court was restricted to just five appearances for the Cherries. When George was forced to miss a game the club displayed notices around the ground on match days informing spectators that he would not be playing. I imagine this was to avoid demands for a refund from those who had paid their admission money just to see George.

George Best

22 May 1946

25 November 2005